"What moves me most about *In Bibi's Kitchen* is Hawa Hassan's connection with these admirable women whose cooking traditions serve their families and help define their communities at home and abroad. I am thankful to see their faces, to meet them in their own words, and to know them and their diverse cultures far beyond the stifling generalities that America so often wields to conflate African people. This book illustrates what the wisest among us have known all along: The seat of power in food—its soul and expertise—has always begun at home, at the hands of skilled women in their kitchens."

   —Osayi Endolyn, James Beard Award–winning writer

"*In Bibi's Kitchen* is rooted in tradition and reverence, but carries forth its stories with an urgency and energy that feels brand new. The book's tenderly reported interviews and East African recipes shine a light on a group who must be seen, must be heard from. Of course we all need more bibis in our lives. And we need the ones in these pages more now than ever. *In Bibi's Kitchen* is an inimitable accomplishment and an essential read that will enrich kitchens and souls everywhere it lands."

   —Howie Kahn, *New York Times* bestselling author,
   James Beard Award winner, and host of *Take Away Only*

What Is a Bibi?

Bibi means "grandmother" in Swahili, an original African language that is the most universally spoken language in East Africa, where an estimated hundred million people speak it.

We use the Swahili word for grandmother because Swahili is the language that unites the diverse range of cultures from countries featured in this book. Use of the word *bibi* immediately centers the book you're holding on the grandmothers featured in it and celebrates them in their own words. We also use "Ma" as an honorific (just as you might call someone Miss So-and-So).

IN
Bibi's Kitchen

Iconi, Grande Comore

HAWA HASSAN WITH JULIA TURSHEN

IN
Bibi's Kitchen

The Recipes & Stories
of Grandmothers from the
Eight African Countries
That Touch the Indian Ocean

Photographs by Khadija M. Farah & Jennifer May

Illustrations by Araki Koman

TEN SPEED PRESS
California | New York

CONTENTS

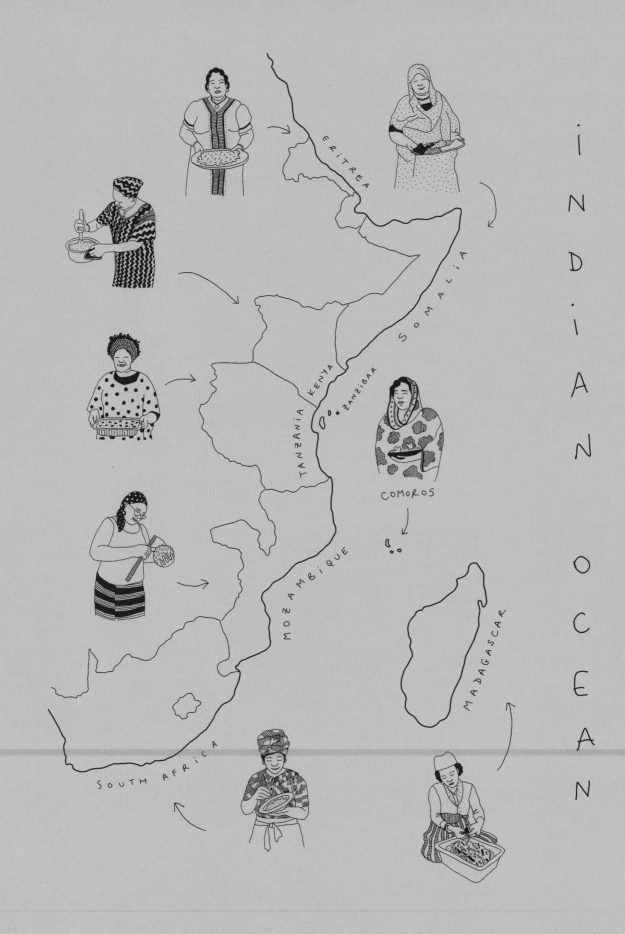

ERITREA

SOMALIA

TANZANIA

KENYA

ZANZIBAR

COMOROS

MOZAMBIQUE

MADAGASCAR

SOUTH AFRICA

INDIAN OCEAN

INTRODUCTION

A Bit About the Book

These pages hold recipes and stories from the kitchens of bibis (grandmothers) from eight African countries that border the Indian Ocean. Their recipes and stories capture the cultural trade winds and flavors from all those who've passed through these countries over the centuries and from the many who remain. In many ways, this is an old-fashioned cookbook that has nothing to do with trends or newness. It's filled with recipes from grandmothers and their rich histories, which have been handed down through generations. It reflects on times that have passed. Yet in so many ways this is an incredibly modern book that has relied on a web of technology and social connections to come together (including, but not limited to, multiple iPhones, many WhatsApp group chats, dozens of Dropbox folders, and countless text messages). This is a book about connection, about multigenerational connection, cross-cultural connection, wireless connection (!), and, ultimately, human connection.

"Food is . . . just like language. For me, stopping traditions would almost be like throwing my culture away," Ma Khanyisa, a grandmother from South Africa, told us. She said this from her home in Cape Town over Skype to Hawa, who was interviewing her and recording the interview before sending it over to Julia (more about us, Hawa and Julia, in a moment). Julia transcribed the interview and added it to the manuscript for the book you're holding, taking note of that line, feeling it to be the crux of this book. Later that week, Khadija M. Farah (more about her soon, too) photographed Ma Khanyisa at her home in South Africa, making corn porridge with a mixture of wild greens known as imifino (check out the recipe on page 211). Khadija also used her phone to film Ma Khanyisa cooking the dish, at times holding her phone in one hand and her camera in the other. She sent the videos to Julia, who wrote the recipe for imifino by watching the videos and then writing down each step that Ma Khanyisa had taken. (Julia has spent over a decade writing cookbooks and can eyeball a tablespoon from a mile away.) There was lots of rewinding to make sure no part of the process had been missed. Then Julia and Hawa tested the written recipes in their own homes to make sure the dishes would translate to Western kitchens.

Variations of this process were repeated for all the grandmothers you're about to meet in these pages. Many live in the eight countries we cover, some left their homes in difficult times and now live in the United States, while Ma Sahra (see page 69) lives in the same place she was born, but because the border has since shifted, her birthplace, once part of Somalia, is now recognized as Kenya. This complicated content-gathering was at times confusing (and at times frustrating when files got stuck in the "cloud" somewhere between continents), but during the entire time, we were all driven to keep speaking this language of food and to make sure traditions and cultures were honored.

In Bibi's Kitchen is not about what is new and next. It's about sustaining a cultural legacy and seeing how food and recipes keep cultures intact, whether those cultures stay in the same place or are displaced. By celebrating bibis and their cooking, we aim to use food as a way to honor the matriarchs of numerous families and countries. And this isn't just any old book with fun ideas of what to make for dinner (though you should make the recipes—they're great!). It's also a collection of stories about war, loss, migration, refuge, and sanctuary. It's a book about families and their connections to home.

This book fills a deep and vast void in the contemporary cookbook market. There are barely any cookbooks published by American publishing houses that feature African food, let alone food from one of the many parts of that continent (disturbingly, Africa is often mistaken as a country, not a continent). On top of that, so many cookbooks are written and photographed by authors and photographers who are not from the places featured in cookbooks and who are unable to bring the richness and complexities of those cultures to the page. On top of that, few cookbooks, or any books, for that matter, champion women who have lived long enough to have grandchildren. We are so happy to tell the stories of these bibis.

And the eight countries we focus on? Eritrea, Somalia, Kenya, Tanzania, Mozambique, South Africa, Madagascar, and Comoros—they all touch the Indian Ocean, some just on an eastern edge, while others are completely surrounded by water (Madagascar and Comoros are islands just east of Mozambique). That they all have the Indian Ocean in common means that they're eight countries bound by trade, by veritable waves of commerce.

Most notably, these eight countries define the backbone of the spice trade, many of them exporters of essential ingredients like pepper and vanilla. We can understand their economic histories, as it were, by learning about their recipes. As interest in "global flavors" continues to gain momentum, it's important to do the work of understanding the culture and people behind those flavors and what they've been through. It's important to understand how these foods have traveled and evolved from small regions across distant oceans to kitchens as far away as ours in New York.

These eight countries also tell a range of stories, and in sharing the bibis' most favorite recipes, we also learn of the lasting effects of colonialism, even in countries that have maintained independence for decades. The late author Laurie Colwin once wrote, "If you want to know what *real* life used to be like, meaning domestic life, there isn't anywhere you can go that gives you a better idea than a cookbook." Examining a country's best-known dishes tells us about so much more than just its popular flavors. It tells you about that country's geography and climate, about farming and distribution, and about those who live there and what their day-to-day life might look and taste like. It also tells you a lot about who holds power and influence.

Consider, for example, that one of the most popular dishes in Somalia is spaghetti. Even though Somalia has the longest coastline on the African continent's mainland and grows tropical produce like bananas, the lasting effect of Italian influence means that you're as likely to find pasta for dinner in a Somali's home as you are a traditional stew such as Digaag Qumbe (Chicken Stew with Yogurt and Coconut, page 73). We can see a very similar Portuguese influence in Mozambique (check out the Piri Piri Sauce, page 185), the lasting effects of the French in Comoros (like the technique employed in the sauce served on the Grilled Lobster Tails with Vanilla Sauce, page 269), and the mark of British customs in Kenya (look no further than the absence of spices in dishes like Ma Wambui's Mukimo with Onions and Greens, page 124).

A Bit More About Us

We promised we'd explain more about ourselves—well, here we are! We're Hawa Hassan and Julia Turshen, two friends whose backgrounds could not be more different but who have been brought together through a shared love of food and all the meaning that brings along. We also share a few beliefs. We believe that food connects the dots. We believe that grandmothers hold the world's most important stories. We believe that home cooking is where culture is created and sustained. We believe that collecting these stories from the bibis we are lucky to know will not just help to cement their legacy, but will also create new traditions for you and your families. We believe that when you read their stories and make their recipes, you will carry their torches.

Hawa was born in Mogadishu, Somalia, in a time of a raging civil war. With the civil war progressing, at the tender age of four, she and her family fled Somalia to settle in a UN refugee camp in neighboring Kenya. While transitioning to this new life in Kenya, she watched her mother work miracles in that difficult environment to keep the family safe, fed, and educated. When Hawa was seven, fate intervened and she was given the opportunity to join a group of Somali refugees who had space for a little girl on their way to being resettled to Seattle, Washington. Seeing an opportunity for her eldest daughter to go to America, Hawa's mother made the difficult decision to send her alone with the hope her mother and four siblings would soon follow. Ultimately, they were never given the chance to reconnect and it would be fifteen years before Hawa would see her mother and siblings in person again, but this time in Norway where her mother finally settled.

It took Hawa a few years to accept and internalize that no one from her family would join her in Seattle. As a means of survival, she became determined to make friends, to culturally assimilate, and to form her own community in her new home. She turned to playing group sports to meet others, learning to use basketball as more than just an activity but also as a means of connection. Hawa eventually moved in with an American teammate's family, leaving the Somali refugees she had come with. Over time, building on this new set of connections led to her becoming more distant from her Somali culture, barely speaking to her extended family, having few Somali friends, or eating Somali food, for a number of years.

After high school, Hawa began modeling and moved to New York City to further her career. It was in this time that she finally bought a ticket to Oslo, Norway, to see her mother and siblings where they had resettled and made a new life with her mother having opened two local stores. While she was waiting at the airport in Oslo for her mother to pick her up, Hawa immediately recognized her mother in an approaching car. Her mother exclaimed, "You recognize me! You recognize me!"

When they got back to her mother's home, Hawa and her mother immediately resumed the mother-daughter roles that she distantly remembered. Hawa stepped back into the treasured memories she kept of being her mother's helper, huddling around the stove cooking dishes like Canjeero (Sourdough Pancakes, page 83), Bariis (Basmati Rice Pilaf with Raisins, page 87), and Suugo Suqaar (Pasta Sauce with Beef, page 90). The shared time cooking gave them a familiar setting to reconnect, to catch up with one another, to meet each other anew, and to feel a connection to their now-distant home.

After that first trip, Hawa returned frequently to Oslo and slowly regained the closeness of family and familiarity with her Somali culture that had been suppressed after many years of assimilation in the United States. This allowed her not only to know her family better, but also to better understand herself, to feel more grounded in her historical roots, and to understand herself in a cultural arc. Now she knew where her loud voice came from, the source of her sometimes fiery temper while haggling for better prices at her local food markets, and where her urge to eat sweet bananas with savory food came from. She had found her people, she had found a connection to home.

After modeling in New York for almost a decade, Hawa packed her bags and went to Oslo for an extended stay, a place she had now become comfortable with and considered a home. Among the few items she packed, she brought her never-failing blender. She thought she'd work on recipes to start a natural juice business, given her interest in all things natural. She kept using her blender to make her traditional Somali basbaas sauce, a blend of chile peppers and other seasonings that she refers to as "Somali ketchup," since Somalis put it on everything. That's when a light bulb went off. There were enough people in America already making juice, but this Somali sauce could offer something unique in the growing culinary milieu that was embracing ethnic flavors and changing the American palette. She started tweaking her mother's recipes to fit American tastes and ingredients, and in 2015, Hawa's company, Basbaas, was officially born.

For Hawa, food both anchors her to her ever shifting notions of home, as well as allows her to bridge the many contexts and locales of her personal journey. It is a powerful language that enables her to share herself and her story far and wide, and to form that universal connection with others longing for a connection to home. Equally important, a core mission of Basbaas is to use food to help shift and extend the existing narrative about Somalia in America from a story mainly of refugees, loss, and sadness, to one about resilience, entrepreneurship, and an incredibly diverse culture once at the crossroads of the spice trade. Food lets us all tell stories about ourselves in ways that are at once unique and relatable. Since basbaas is always homemade in Somali kitchens, and Hawa's basbaas is the first ready-made version available anywhere in the United States, she is not only able to introduce new flavors but to help Americans better understand and explore the diversity and history of Somalia's cuisine as well as that of various other African cuisines.

Julia was born in Manhattan to two Jewish New Yorkers and cannot remember a time when she wasn't drawn like a magnet to the kitchen. Her love of food, cooking, and community is inherited. Julia's maternal grandparents, a baker's daughter and a flour miller's son, fled Eastern Europe during the pogroms. Once her grandparents found refuge in the United States in the early 1920s, they moved to New York, where they opened a bread bakery in Brooklyn and where Julia's mother and aunts grew up. Julia's paternal great-grandparents ran a grain mill in Connecticut (there's gluten in Julia's blood), and when they couldn't find a synagogue in the area, Julia's grandfather built one himself.

Julia has worked on many cookbooks, both her own and others that she's coauthored, and she is passionate about writing reliable recipes for home cooks, so they can be calm in the kitchen and empowered to cook for their families and communities. She brought her experience to this book, so you can be assured that you can make every recipe in these pages at home, whoever and wherever you are.

And the photographers. Khadija M. Farah is an East African native who served as the intrepid in-the-field photographer, bringing out the spirit of the bibis in all of her beautiful images. She traveled through the countries along the Indian Ocean just as traders once did to trade the very spices these stories are based on. Seeing the bibis through Khadija's lens reminds us how important it is not only to highlight women's stories but also to consider who captures and narrates them. It was important to the authors that a male gaze, especially a white male gaze, was never part of the production of this book. Khadija is not only a talented photographer, but she is also a young Muslim Kenyan woman. She offered the bibis a familiarity we could not have found with anyone else; this helped them to feel comfortable sharing their tales and recipes.

And an ocean away in Woodstock, New York, Jennifer May helped bring the rest of the recipes to life in her kitchen studio. She took such a sincere interest in the book and in the bibis' stories that she began reading novels set in East Africa and did her own research to bring these stories and recipes to life.

A Bit More About the Book

This book is organized by country. The order of the chapters follows the Indian Ocean from the northeastern part of Africa, known as the Horn of Africa (Eritrea and Somalia), then hugs the Indian Ocean to the south and lands in Kenya, Tanzania, Mozambique, and South Africa and also includes the majestic islands of Madagascar and Comoros. Each chapter includes an introduction that tells about the history of each country and includes portraits of the bibis.

We've included short interviews with each bibi so you can learn more about them and the role they play in their countries' legacies and traditions. It was important to us that we never speak on their behalf but rather give them space to tell their own stories in their own words. Since each chapter includes at least one bibi and most have a few, each chapter is not only rooted in a specific place but also offers a range of perspectives that clearly illustrate how food changes when it travels and how it can also help to keep a connection to home. Recipes follow each bibi interview, and each recipe is a lesson in tradition, creativity, resourcefulness, history, and/or innovation.

All the recipes you are holding are from women who are home cooks. This book celebrates home cooking and isn't about a professional or cheffy approach to embellish traditional dishes. When asked why they chose whatever recipe they shared, almost every bibi said it was because it was something that was easy to make. This is home cooking, which means you can make everything yourself with widely available and affordable ingredients. Many of the recipes are also vegetarian, if not vegan. This is all to say: you are holding a collection of healthy, cookable recipes that we hope you will bring into your home and cook for your community.

Before the chapters kick off, you'll find a robust pantry and equipment list that breaks down any of the ingredients that might be unfamiliar to you and lets you know where to find them (and what to substitute if you can't find them). We hope anything that's new will excite you as much as it has excited us and help you incorporate recipes and ingredients from places you might not yet have been. *In Bibi's Kitchen* aims to be a tool that serves food's highest purpose: to connect us all.

Most of all, we cannot wait for you to meet each of the bibis. In the pages that follow, you'll meet women such as Ma Wambui in Nairobi, who used to be a caterer, and Ma Shara in Zanzibar, who teaches cooking classes for visiting tourists so they can "see the real Zanzibar." You'll see women like Ma Mariama in Comoros who cook outdoors in rustic kitchens, where each meal starts with building a fire, and others, like Ma Josefina in Mozambique, who cook in kitchens that probably look a lot like yours.

In the United States, you'll meet bibis like Ma Vicky, a real-life princess from Tanzania who now lives in suburban New York. She makes a mean matoke (stewed plantains with beans and beef, page 150), as well her signature lasagna (page 156), her family's all-time favorite dish that speaks as much to the Italian influence in East Africa as it does to her family's Tanzanian American diasporic experience. In her cooking, Ma Vicky reminds us how food can be a bridge to home, even if home is very far away. Being in the kitchens with so many women was a beautiful experience of trust. When a bibi gives you her recipe, she gives you her story.

In creating this book, we have come to understand more than ever that we all have more in common than separates us. Even in celebrating all the things that make us distinct, both as people and as nations, we found over and over again that no matter where we go, women are the ones sustaining their families and communities, and food is the main tool of that literal and figurative sustenance. Wherever there is a community, there's likely a knowing woman stirring a pot.

Making this book has also reminded us of one of the most universal truths: we all just want to be seen and heard. Being acknowledged makes us feel part of a community and also endows us with a sense of pride. When Hawa and Khadija visited Eritrean-born Ma Gehennet at her home in Yonkers, New York (about 20 minutes outside of New York City), she proudly showed them her tea collection, built of gifts that her children have brought her from their travels. "They know what I like," she said, after telling us that the thing she is most proud of is being their mom. She gave Hawa each tea to smell, beaming with pride. We hope that in meeting the bibis in this book, you think of your own elders and what they mean to you, how they've made you feel recognized, and what you can do to help make them feel seen in turn.

PANTRY: INGREDIENTS AND EQUIPMENT

When we've told friends and family about this book, they've asked if the recipes will require unusual ingredients or hard-to-find equipment. We're so happy to report that the bibis' recipes can all be made with ingredients and equipment that are probably already in your kitchen.

Spices and Seasonings

The recipes in this book come from or are inspired by women who cook at home on a regular basis; this means they're all easy to prepare in your own kitchen. The thing that sets many of them apart from the dishes you might already have in your repertoire are the spices. Spices take ordinary ingredients like vegetables and beans from a place of nothing-to-write-home-about to something-to-write-about-in-a-book. And getting to know the following spices and seasonings will put the food of the African countries that touch the Indian Ocean within your reach. They're not difficult to come by, especially if you have a shop with a good spice selection in your area (be sure to seek out any specialty grocery stores that feature goods from places like Africa, India, or Asia). If you can't find them locally, they're all available online. Our favorite sources include Kalustyan's (foodsofnations.com), Burlap & Barrel (burlapandbarrel.com), Diaspora Co. (diasporaco.com) for turmeric and cardamom, and Spicewalla (spicewallabrand.com).

ADOBO SEASONING. You'll find adobo seasoning in both of Ma Vicky's recipes: Matoke with Steamed Spinach (Stewed Plantains with Pink Beans, Beef, and Coconut Milk, page 150) and Ma Vicky's Famous Lasagna (page 156). Adobo is a blend of spices that almost always includes garlic powder, salt, pepper, and often paprika and oregano. There are plenty of variations and brands, but Goya, the most widely available one, is the one Ma Vicky reaches for. The name adobo has its roots in the Spanish verb *adobar*, which means "to marinate." Ma Vicky uses it for the same reason so many other cooks and chefs do: it's a shortcut to lots of flavor. If you make one of her recipes and don't have adobo, simply substitute half kosher salt and half garlic powder.

ALLSPICE BERRIES. Allspice berries taste like a mix between cinnamon, cloves, and nutmeg. Also known as pimento, allspice is native to Mexico and Central America but is now grown in warm climates across the world, including East Africa. It's a central flavor in Jamaican cooking, and the berries are often used in pickling. While some recipes use whole allspice berries, ground allspice is used in the Denningvleis (Sweet-and-Sour Braised Lamb with Tamarind, page 208). If you can't find allspice,

substitute two-thirds cinnamon and one-third cloves (whole or ground, depending on the recipe).

BOUILLON CUBES. Quite a few recipes in this book use bouillon cubes. From Ma Gehennet's Zebhi Hamli (Stewed Spinach, page 44) to Ma Vicky's Famous Lasagna (page 156) and Ma Kauthar's Chicken Biryani (page 122), bouillon cubes are a fast and easy way to add the flavor of stock to whatever you're cooking, without going to the trouble of making stock. We tested the recipes using Maggi-brand bouillon cubes, since that's what many of the bibis used, but whatever brand you like will work; feel free to use chicken or vegetable, depending on your preferences and dietary needs. If you don't have (or don't like to use) bouillon cubes, simply substitute half kosher salt and half garlic powder (use a teaspoon each for every 2 cups of stock).

CARDAMOM. Cardamom has a warm, distinctive flavor that is hard to substitute. Luckily, it's widely available (check the sources we mentioned at the beginning of this section, if needed). Although cardamom is expensive, a little bit goes a very long way. Some recipes use whole cardamom pods, others use crushed pods, and some use ground cardamom (ground from the seeds inside the cardamom pods). Cardamom pods come in green and black (the green pods are fresher; the black ones are aged).

We like green cardamom pods, since they're more readily available than the black ones and have a milder, almost sweeter flavor.

CINNAMON. We use whole cinnamon sticks in lots of recipes as well as ground cinnamon. Cinnamon's warm, almost sweet flavor brings dimension to so many recipes, from spice blends like the Xawaash Spice Mix (page 74) from Somalia to rice dishes like Zanzibar Pilau (Rice Pilaf, page 148) from Tanzania and Ma Kauthar's Chicken Biryani (page 122) from Kenya.

CLOVES. Native to Indonesia, cloves appear whole and ground in plenty of the recipes in this book and offer their warm, slightly spicy flavor wherever they go, whether in Iced Rooibos Tea with Orange, Cloves, and Cinnamon (page 214) from South Africa or Bariis (Basmati Rice Pilaf with Raisins, page 87) from Somalia. Like many spices, cloves also have medicinal qualities and have been used in holistic medicine for ages, especially for dental care.

CORIANDER. Coriander seeds eventually grow into the plant called cilantro. We use the seeds both whole and ground in various recipes and love their tart flavor. Even if you're part of the small percentage of the population that thinks cilantro tastes like dish soap (it's a genetic thing!), the seeds don't usually have that same effect. If you can't find (or don't like) coriander seeds or ground coriander, feel free to substitute an equal measure of cumin seeds or ground cumin in its place.

CUMIN. Where would so many dishes be without cumin? We don't want to know! Cumin is used throughout the world and is as central to East African cooking as it is to Indian, Mexican, and Middle Eastern cooking. You'll see cumin seeds in lots of recipes and ground cumin in others. The plant is part of the parsley family. Widely available, you should have no trouble finding it. If for any reason you really dislike it, feel free to use a little less than the amount called for or substitute an equal amount of coriander seeds or ground coriander.

FENUGREEK SEEDS. Fenugreek seeds are dark yellow and cuboid-shaped and impart a sweet flavor, so much so that fenugreek's taste and aroma have been likened to maple syrup. In fact, in 2005, the smell of maple syrup overwhelmed Lower Manhattan, and it was reported in many local newspapers and media. The source? A factory in nearby New Jersey that was processing fenugreek. Too much fenugreek in your cooking can make things taste bitter, so remember, a little goes a long way. We use it in the Berbere Spice Mix (page 50); feel free to use the seeds in other dishes like dals and even in pickles—the seeds are also great in brine, combined with other spices like allspice berries. If you can't find fenugreek seeds for the Berbere Spice Mix, you can simply leave them out.

GINGER. Wonderfully spicy, fragrant, and distinctive, ginger, whether fresh (see page 21) or dried, is central to so many recipes in this book. Dried ginger is the same as ground ginger and is widely available in most grocery stores; it has a milder flavor than fresh ginger. It adds warmth to Ma Shara's Spiced Fried Fish (page 153) and other recipes. Whole dried ginger, which is less commonly available (but check over at Kalustyan's, foodsofnations.com), is what makes Ma Gehennet's Buna (Eritrean Coffee, page 54) so special. She grinds it with her freshly roasted coffee beans to make a sum somehow greater than its parts. Ground ginger can be used in its place.

NUTMEG. Nutmeg is really just a large, dried seed and has a wonderfully sweet flavor that goes as well in baked goods as it does in savory dishes (it pairs especially nicely with dairy). We love its savory-sweet impact on Ndizi Kaanga (Fried Plantains, page 145). We prefer buying whole nutmeg seeds and then grinding them as needed using a Microplane. You can also buy ground nutmeg, but the flavor of freshly grated is really exceptional. [Fun fact: Mace, a nutmeg-ish spice that has a more delicate flavor, comes from the seed covering of nutmeg.]

PEPPER. Pepper is so often called for in recipes without regard to its intense flavor. A spice like any other, black pepper adds an earthy heat wherever it goes. We use whole black peppercorns in expected places like the Xawaash Spice Mix (page 74) and in more unexpected places like Shaah Cadays (Somali Spiced Tea with Milk, page 94), where pepper adds dimension to the sweet tea. Freshly ground black pepper is called for in a number of recipes, too. We also use dried whole chile peppers and sweet paprika, which is its own type of ground chile pepper, in one recipe, the Berbere Spice Mix (page 50). Otherwise, chile is used as a fresh ingredient (that is, jalapeños, habaneros, and so on). In general, if you can't find the specific type of fresh chile pepper we call for, substitute whatever you can get and always feel free to use more if you like things extra hot, or less (or none at all) if you prefer your food to be milder.

SALT. All recipes use kosher salt since it's neutral in flavor, easy to measure, and widely available. The Diamond Crystal brand was used in the testing of all the recipes in this book. If you use another brand, such as Morton's, start with half the quantity called for, since some brands are saltier than others and it's far easier to add more salt to a recipe than to subtract it. One recipe, Ma Penny's Sautéed Cabbage (page 117), uses seasoned salt—our preferred brand is Lawry's (widely available in grocery stores). If you can't find Lawry's, mix equal parts kosher salt, garlic powder, and paprika.

STAR ANISE. Ma Kauthar's Chicken Biryani (page 122) is the only recipe that uses star anise, a spice native to Vietnam and China. Ma Kauthar uses it to flavor the rice for the biryani; you might recognize its flavor from pho, the Vietnamese soup. If you don't have star anise, feel free to leave it out of the recipe, since there's already loads of flavor from the cinnamon and cardamom.

GROUND TURMERIC. Turmeric is from the same family as ginger. When this rhizome is dried and ground, the resulting spice is recognizable for its rich orange color. Ground turmeric, like many of the spices used in this book, has a warm flavor and is very earthy tasting. It's like a cross between black pepper, ground mustard, and ginger. It's available in most grocery stores but is best sourced from a reputable spice vendor like Diaspora Co. (diasporaco.com), since the fresher the turmeric, the better the flavor (it's also great to support businesses like Diaspora Co. that are invested in building a better spice trade). We use ground turmeric in so many recipes, like the Xawaash Spice Mix (page 74) from Somalia, and for seasoning simple meat dishes like Ma Halima's Beef Suqaar (page 84). In fact, when we were photographing many of the food photos at Jen May's studio in Woodstock, New York, all the turmeric we cooked with over those wonderful days caused her wooden spoon to be dyed yellow.

VANILLA. Vanilla is one of the most commonly enjoyed flavors and scents in the world, and also one of the most imitated. Real vanilla, not the imitation stuff, actually comes from specific types of orchids (how cool is that?). Madagascar produces most of the world's vanilla supply (it's estimated at about 80 percent). Whole vanilla pods have to be harvested, dried, and aged before they arrive in our kitchens. Vanilla extract is made by macerating the vanilla pods in alcohol. You can make your own extract by submerging pods in vodka or bourbon, which is especially great for getting all the flavor possible from the pods, after you've scraped out the tiny beans inside them for your cooking and baking. You can also put scraped pods into a jar of sugar and let them sit there indefinitely; they will infuse the sugar with their flavor and fragrance. While saffron remains the most expensive spice in the world, vanilla is a close second. You don't need much of the good stuff, though, to taste it in your food. It's best to buy from a company that sources vanilla responsibly. We get ours from Kalustyan's (foodsofnations.com).

Dry, Canned, and Bottled Goods

A well-stocked pantry will put all the recipes in this book within your reach, quite literally. Nearly all the ingredients we call for are available in most national grocery chains, but there are a few ingredients worth shouting out here with some notes and sources.

BEANS AND LEGUMES. So many recipes in this collection are healthy, vegetarian or vegan, and also affordable. And the key to so many of them? Beans and legumes. Full of fiber and protein and able to sit in your pantry for long periods of time, beans and legumes are one of the best ways to spend and stretch a dollar in your cooking (plus, they're way better for the environment than meat). Whether you're putting pigeon peas in Ambrevades au Curry (Curried Pigeon Peas, page 263), frozen lima beans in Shahan Ful (Mashed Limas with Onions, Tomatoes, and Chiles, page 47), or green split peas in Ma Penny's Mukimo (Mashed Green Split Peas, Corn, and Potatoes, page 118), beans and legumes cross the coastline of the Indian Ocean and the pages of this book. Look for canned beans not only in the canned food aisle of the grocery store but also wherever your store shelves ingredients from Mexico and other Latin American countries.

COCONUT PRODUCTS. Coconut is a very important ingredient in the countries that touch the Indian Ocean. Throughout the book, any recipe calling for full-fat unsweetened coconut milk was tested with canned coconut milk that was shaken vigorously before being opened (if the coconut milk is still separate, pour the contents of the can into a blender and blend until smooth and combined). Aroy-D and Roland are our preferred brands that are readily available in the United States. For coconut oil, we like the flavor that cold-pressed coconut oil delivers. There are many good brands out there, and it's widely available at grocery stores and natural foods stores.

DRIED FRUITS AND NUTS. Whether it's juicy Medjool dates for Date Bread (page 158), raisins in Bariis (Basmati Rice Pilaf with Raisins, page 87), or almonds in Ma Kauthar's Basboosa (Semolina Cake, page 128), dried fruits and nuts add sweetness, richness, and texture to so many recipes. Try to buy your dried fruits and nuts from places with high turnover. We get ours from Kalustyan's (foodsofnations.com).

FLOURS AND CORNMEAL. So many of the breads in this book, like Ma Shara's Ajemi Bread with Carrots and Green Pepper (page 146) and Ma Halima's Sabaayad (Somali Flatbreads, page 76), rely on good-quality flours and cornmeal. All recipes were tested with King Arthur all-purpose flour and whole wheat flour. For the chickpea flour for Ma Gehennet's Shiro (Ground Chickpea Stew, page 45), we used Bob's Red Mill (bobsredmill.com). You can also make your own chickpea flour by grinding dried chickpeas in a high-speed, high-powered blender or an at-home grain mill. Chickpea flour is also readily available in Indian grocery stores, where it is often sold under the name 'besan'. For the finely ground cornmeal in both Canjeero (Sourdough Pancakes, page 83) and Ma Maria's Xima (Smooth Cornmeal Porridge, page 182), we ground regular white cornmeal in a high-speed blender in 10-second bursts until it was more finely ground. You can also source finely ground cornmeal from Bob's Red Mill; that's also where you can find the semolina flour for Ma Kauthar's Basboosa (Semolina Cake, page 128) and the cassava flour for Ma Baomaka's Mofo Akondro (Banana Fritters, page 241). Cassava flour is made from the whole cassava (yuca) root, which is dried and ground. While tapioca flour derives from cassava, it's not the same thing as cassava flour (tapioca is a more processed ingredient and is starchier than cassava flour, almost like cornstarch versus cornmeal). Cassava flour is entirely gluten- and grain-free and has therefore become a popular ingredient for modern "wellness" recipe developers. Note that East Africans, as well as many other cultures that rely on cassava, have been hip to its benefits for generations.

GHEE. Ghee is a type of clarified butter. Regular butter consists of butterfat plus milk solids and water. When you remove those extras, the milk solids and the water, you're left with ghee, which has a higher smoke point than butter, so it's better for high-heat cooking—plus, it tastes extremely rich (almost like buttered popcorn). You can buy ghee in jars at the store (we like the store brand from Kalustyan's, foodsofnations.com), or you can easily make your own. To make about 1½ cups ghee, start with 1 pound (that's four sticks) high-quality unsalted butter. Line a

strainer with a coffee filter and set it over a large bowl. Cut the butter into small pieces and place them in a saucepan over high heat. Once the butter melts, let it cook for a few minutes, until the milk solids float, then reduce the heat and let the butter cook for a few more minutes, until the milk solids sink to the bottom and turn golden brown (this adds flavor to the ghee). Turn off the heat and pour the butter through the strainer. Discard the contents of the strainer; what you're left with in the bowl, that beautiful golden liquid, is your ghee. Let it cool to room temperature and then store it in a jar or airtight container in the refrigerator for up to a year. It will solidify in the refrigerator (just like regular butter).

TAMARIND PASTE. Intensely tart with a depth of flavor, tamarind paste is an essential component of Denningvleis (Sweet-and-Sour Braised Lamb with Tamarind, page 208). If you can't find tamarind paste, you can substitute an equal amount of sherry vinegar or fresh lemon juice in the stew (or try a combination of the two). Be sure to look for sour tamarind paste, not sweet tamarind paste (meaning, buy paste that lists tamarind as the only ingredient, not sugar, too). If you find tamarind paste that still has seeds in it, simply mix the paste with a little bit of boiling water to loosen it and then separate the seeds from the paste with your fingers and discard the seeds. If you have leftover paste, mix it with sugar to taste, roll it into small balls, and then roll it in more sugar. Store the balls in an airtight container in the refrigerator and serve with tea or just enjoy as a snack—it's like a homemade sweet-and-sour candy.

TEA AND GREEN COFFEE BEANS. The two types of tea used in this book, black tea for Shaah Cadays (Somali Spiced Tea with Milk, page 94) and rooibos for Iced Rooibos Tea with Orange, Cloves, and Cinnamon (page 214), are widely available in grocery stores and tea shops. Our favorite online source is McNulty's (mcnultys.com), the storied store on Christopher Street in Manhattan's West Village. For the green coffee beans for Ma Gehennet's Buna (Eritrean Coffee, page 54), the best online source we've found is the Coffee Bean Corral (coffeebeancorral.com).

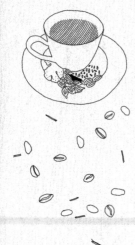

YEAST. Every recipe requiring yeast in this book, such as Ma Shara's Ajemi Bread with Carrots and Green Pepper (page 146) and Canjeero (Sourdough Pancakes, page 83), uses active dry yeast. We find it to be the most commonly available type of yeast in American grocery stores. Unlike instant yeast (also sometimes labeled rapid-rise yeast), which can just be mixed with all of the dough ingredients at once, active dry yeast needs to be dissolved in liquid before being mixed into any dough (and that's what you'll see as the first step of each recipe that calls for yeast). This also means that if you accidentally use instant yeast, you'll still be good to go. Look for envelopes or small jars of active dry yeast in the baking aisle of the grocery store. If you don't find it there, look in the refrigerated aisle (it does not have to be refrigerated, but it doesn't hurt). Whatever type of yeast you're using, be sure to check the date on the package to ensure it's still fresh.

Fresh and Frozen Ingredients

Most of the fresh ingredients called for in the recipes are readily available (like onions, garlic, carrots, and peppers). Here are a few notes on four ingredients that you might not find in your local grocery store.

FROZEN JUMBO CORN KERNELS (OFTEN LABELED CHOCLO DESGRANADO). There are two recipes in the Kenya chapter for mukimo, a healthy and affordable mixture of mashed potatoes, large corn kernels, and either green split peas or pureed greens. One is from Ma Penny (see page 118), who lives in Massachusetts, and the other is from Ma Wambui, who lives in Nairobi (see page 124). For these recipes, you need extremely large corn kernels that are starchy, and not the small, sweet frozen corn kernels more commonly found in supermarkets. We have found that the Goya brand of frozen jumbo corn kernels, labeled Choclo Desgranado, are the best for both mukimos. Look for the corn kernels in the freezer aisle of the grocery store near other Goya products. If you can't find them in your grocery store, go to a store that serves a Latinx population. Drained and rinsed canned hominy also works well.

GINGER. Fresh ginger adds so much amazing flavor to every dish it's used in. To peel your ginger, use a small spoon (like one you'd eat cereal with) to scrape off the ginger's thin skin, instead of using a vegetable peeler or a paring knife (both usually end up taking off a lot of the ginger itself). The spoon will take off the brown skin and nothing else. This is a great job to give a child who's in the kitchen with you since it doesn't require using a sharp tool—plus, there's the instant reward of seeing the ginger transform from dry to fragrant and juicy.

PLANTAINS. Part of the banana family but starchier, larger, and lower in sugar, plantains appear in so many recipes in this book. Just like bananas, there are tons of varietals of plantains in the world (and many are available in Africa), but American grocery stores carry only one main type and offer them in either green or yellow. The green ones are fresher, starchier, and drier than the yellow ones, which are riper and sweeter. We use only yellow ones in Ndizi Kaanga (Fried Plantains, page 145), because we want their sweetness in that preparation (if you can only find green ones, let them ripen on your counter for a few days and watch them turn yellow). Otherwise, green plantains are used throughout the book in dishes like Ma Vicky's Matoke with Steamed Spinach (Stewed Plantains with Pink Beans, Beef, and Coconut Milk, page 150) and Ma Mariama's M'tsolola (Fish, Yuca, Green Plantain, and Coconut Milk Stew, page 266). Look for plantains near the bananas in your grocery store or near the Latin American ingredients. If you can't find them in your grocery store, go to a store that serves a Latinx population.

YUCA (CASSAVA). Yuca, sometimes labeled cassava, is a nutty-flavored, starchy root vegetable that's almost like a very firm potato. It must be cooked before eating—it can be poisonous if eaten raw. It grows in subtropical climates and is one of the most widely consumed foods in the world, since it grows well and offers a lot of nutrition. It's also very versatile and can be boiled, mashed, fried, and more. We use it in recipes like Ma Mariama's M'tsolola (Fish, Yuca, Green Plantain, and Coconut Milk Stew, page 266). Before cooking yuca, use a sharp knife to peel off its tough brown skin, then prepare the flesh according to the recipe directions.

Equipment

You don't need any unusual or highly specific equipment to make any recipe in this book. The only exception is a jebena, a traditional coffeepot, which we use to make Ma Gehennet's Buna (Eritrean Coffee, page 54). You can find beautiful ones online through sites like eBay and Etsy, but as we talk about in the recipe, while it is traditional to use a jebena, it's okay if you don't have one. The recipe is really a reminder of the power of using food and drink as a ritual and as a way to gather your community. It's also a reminder of how wonderful freshly roasted coffee is!

Otherwise, the only equipment beyond standard kitchen stuff (like a sharp knife, a cutting board, bowls, a colander and/or a sieve, and regular pots and pans) that we occasionally call for are tools to help grind things and break them down. This means, at times, a blender, a food processor, and sometimes an electric coffee grinder or a mortar and pestle to grind spices. We are specific about when to use a blender versus a food processor in many places because a blender is better for mixtures that include a lot of liquid and helps makes things very smooth, whereas a food processor does a better job of finely chopping things. If you only have one of those machines, don't run to a store to buy the other. Just use what you have—it will all be fine. And if you're grinding spices and don't have a coffee grinder or a mortar and pestle, put the spices in a plastic bag, press out the air and seal the bag, then crush the spices with the bottom of a heavy pot or with a rolling pin. There's always a way.

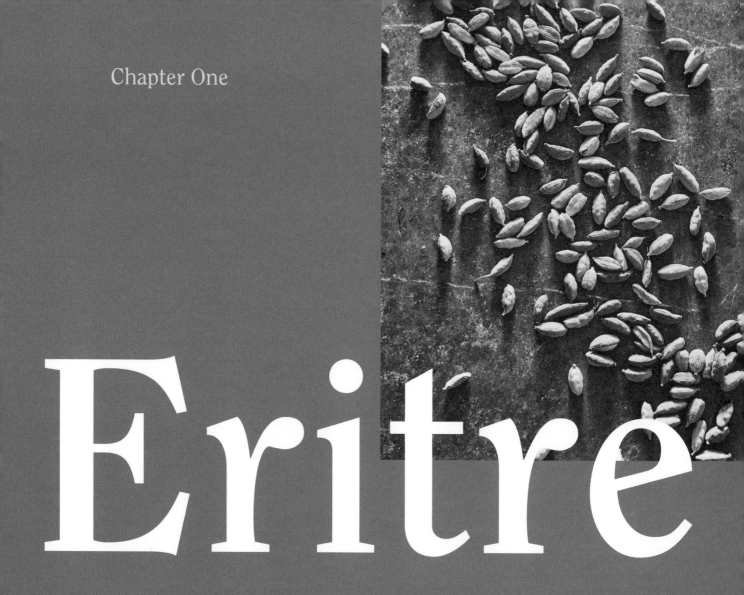

Eritre

a

Part of the Horn of Africa, Eritrea is a varied country with nine recognized ethnic groups, with multiple languages spoken and religions practiced. Formerly part of the Abyssinia empire, along with Ethiopia, the country was first called Eritrea in 1890, when Italy colonized the area and named it after the Greek name for the Red Sea. (The name remained even after the British and subsequently Ethiopia took control; it persisted even after the country gained independence in 1993.) Eritrea's coastline extends along the Red Sea, an inlet of the Indian Ocean. In looking at the food cooked in Eritrea, we can see a distinctive mixture of Indian, Arab, and Ethiopian influences.

To say there's history in Eritrea would be a massive understatement. The remains of a hominid (meaning a great ape), dated to over one million years old, were found in Eritrea and provide a very possible link in human evolution. Eritrea's roots, in other words, run very deep.

Skipping over a few decades, Eritrea is part of an area that ancient Egyptians called Punt (along with modern-day Djibouti, parts of Somalia and Sudan, and Ethiopia). Artifacts from Ona urban culture, thought to be one of the first populations in the Horn of Africa, dated between 800 and 400 BCE, have been found in Eritrea's highlands. The Middle Ages led way to Ottoman control. Fast-forward again. The boundaries of what we now know as Eritrea were established around 1870 during the European colonial division of Africa known as the Scramble for Africa. During this time, Western Europeans invaded, occupied, and colonized African land and its people.

The first Italian settlers arrived a decade later in 1880. During their control, Italians built the Eritrean Railway, invested in agriculture, and built factories, including ones that produced pasta. After Mussolini rose to power and brought a Fascist regime everywhere he went, Eritrea became the industrial center of Italian East Africa.

The British defeated the Italian army and took power in 1941, following the Battle of Keren, and in the 1950s, Eritrea was federated with Ethiopia. A secessionist movement started soon after, in 1958, led first by the Eritrean Liberation Front (ELF), an organization that pioneered the struggle for Eritrea's independence from Ethiopia. In 1962, Haile

Selassie, the emperor of Ethiopia, dissolved the Eritrean parliament and annexed Eritrea. The Eritrean war for independence went on for the next three decades, until 1991, when the Eritrean People's Liberation Front (EPLF), a splinter group of the ELF, defeated Ethiopian forces. (By 1990, women made up 40 percent of the EPLF—a higher percentage of women than any other liberation army in the world.) In 1993, Eritrea officially gained independence. Currently, the People's Front for Democracy and Justice, the founding political party, exists as the only legal party.

Geography and Climate

Eritrea's eastern coast lies on the Red Sea. Sudan is on its west side, Ethiopia is just south, and Djibouti is to its southeast. The Dahlak Archipelago lies right off Eritrea's coastline. Asmara, the capital, and Asseb, a southeast port town, are the two main cities. Massawa in the east, Mendefera in the center, and Keren in the north are the most populous towns. Its climate is as diverse as its geography. While the highlands are temperate and mild, the lowlands are arid. This climate variation impacts Eritrean agriculture (more grows in the highlands).

Economy and Resources

Resources in Eritrea include gold and silver in the Bisha mine and cement in Massawa. Eritrea is also full of wildlife—there are over 500 types of birds in the country, plus many large animals such as gazelles. The majority of Eritrea's workforce is employed in agriculture. Eritrean agricultural products include grains like millet, barley, wheat, and sorghum; spices like pepper; seeds like linseed and sesame; animals, including goat, sheep, cattle, and camels; and fresh produce.

People

Over half the population of Eritrea identifies as Tigrinya, about a third as Tigre, and the rest as Saho, Kunama, Bilen, Rashaida, and more.

Language

Nationally recognized languages include Tigrinya, Beja, Arabic, Tigre, Kunama, Saho, Bilen, Nara, Afar, and English.

Religion

Over half the Eritrean population practices Christianity, about a third follow Islam, and the remainder practice various indigenous religions, Judaism, Hinduism, Buddhism, and more.

Ma Abeba

HOME
Nairobi, Kenya

HER RECIPE
Firfir (Stewed Injera with Meat, Tomatoes, and Onions, page 48)

Where are you originally from?
A small village called Adi Guadad just outside of the capital city Asmara.

How many kids and grandkids do you have?
I have two daughters and four sons, and I have six granddaughters and two grandsons.

And you and your husband have been married for how long?
Forty-five years.

Why did you choose to make firfir to share with us?
Because it's an easy process, and I eat it almost daily.

What dish do you think best represents Eritrean food?
Dulet.

And what is that?
It's basically like ground beef, but it's not beef. It's from goat, and it includes the intestines and it's ground small and made into a stew. The process isn't easy; it takes time. You need specific ingredients and spices to make it tasty. We make it mostly during holidays or after we've broken a fast.

How often do you cook?

I cook every day and make every meal for my family.

Do your children know how to cook?

They do. My daughter is the only one at home right now, but she helps.

Did you teach her how to cook?

Yes, I did.

What does passing on food traditions mean to you?

It's important to pass it on to my children so the culture can still be there, and they can have the knowledge of the culture.

What does home mean to you?

Adi Guadad. That's where I grew up and had most of my memories. I'd like to go back there eventually. I teach my kids about my past and tell them about how I grew up and tell them about the experiences I had there.

How do you define community?

When I refer to my community specifically, it's about how people from the same place can interact and socialize with each other. Whether you're in Africa or America, you can call yourself a community. Even if you're not home, like back in Eritrea, we over here are able to form a community and feel like we're there.

Looking back, what are you most proud of?

My family. I had the opportunity to grow up in a very happy village, where I was surrounded by family and friends and so many people. I'm a very social person and have so many memories from there. I'm proud I had the opportunity to be surrounded by so many people.

What brought you to Kenya?

There was war in our country, and we had to escape the war, so we came here [to Kenya].

This is during the war with Ethiopia?

Yes, yes. We came here in 1981.

What would you say is most misunderstood about Eritrea?

I don't follow politics or anything like that, but my husband says most people think we don't really depend on ourselves, like we're not developed. But the truth is that we like to work with neighboring countries, Somalia being one of them, so that we can develop ourselves.

So, Eritreans are sometimes thought to be isolated?

Yes, exactly. But we're not.

What was your favorite thing to eat growing up?

Shiro [ground chickpea stew]. My abaye [grandmother] used to make it for me.

Ma Gehennet

HOME
Yonkers, New York

HER RECIPES
Kicha (Eritrean Flatbreads, page 40)

Zebhi Hamli (Stewed Spinach, page 44)

Shiro (Ground Chickpea Stew, page 45)

Buna (Eritrean Coffee, page 54)

How long have you been a preschool teacher?

For over twenty years.

Can you tell us a little bit about your journey from Eritrea to Swaziland to Canada to Yonkers?

Okay, so I was engaged to my husband, about to get married, and then I went to Swaziland at the end of 1982. I stopped in Kenya for one night and stayed with my husband's friends at their house. I spent New Year's Eve of 1983 in Kenya. So, then we went to Swaziland and we had a small wedding. My first son was born New Year's Eve the next year. We were in Swaziland for about four years. We had a daughter. My husband was a project administrator. When our daughter was one and a half and our son was two and a half, we decided to emigrate to Canada. We went through Europe, we met my brother in Italy, and then from there we were in Ottawa. During that time we were emigrating to Canada, my husband was offered a job in New York. He went, and every other weekend he came back to Canada to see us, until I got my papers. My brother was living with me, other family, too, and that's how I did what I did. I finished my education while raising four children, running after school for soccer, for basketball, baseball, for ice skating, swimming, and karate. Boy Scouts. Everything. Ballet. They did everything. I was a full-time mom, and I always brought their friends. We did all of these things, you know. It was busy, but it paid off.

Do your children know how to cook?

Adam does.

Your eldest son?

Yes. He loves to cook. Asgede, too. He doesn't wait for me to make anything for him. He can make it.

What does passing on food traditions mean to you?

When [my children] were young, we always made Eritrean food. And every two years we would go to Eritrea because my husband's job would pay for us to go. So, my kids spoke the language, so whenever they went to Eritrea, they didn't have any problem understanding or eating anything. And people really admired that. They call us 'Adey' (the Tigrinya word for mother) and 'Aboy' (the Tigrinya word for father). My grandbaby calls me 'Abayey' (grandmother) and his auntie 'Amo'. It makes me happy, not just the food, everything. My oldest son can make everything, even our coffee. When he was at NYU, he would have his friends for coffee. They are very proud Eritreans. Knowing the language, knowing the culture, everything helped them. Also going to Eritrea every two years helped them to see how lucky they were to be Americans. They can compare themselves to children in Eritrea, who have enough love and have everything, but of course, Americans are Americans. There's a lot of opportunity here, there's no question about it. So, when my kids would come back, they would work hard and appreciate what they have. It taught them also not to be intimated.

Of their culture?

Yes, yes. Of their roots. To know who they are.

What does home mean to you?

Home means my roots. I don't know how to describe it to you. When we go [to Eritrea], there's peace. I love America; I love my life here. But when we go there, the children can play in the street. We're not worried about them. They are not judged by the color of their skin. They're happier. They are happy. They can go anywhere. It's home. Yeah, it's home.

How do you define community?

It's in the house first. Who comes to the house first? Family.

So, community for you is built in the home?

Yes, it's the people who shape the children. The most important is the extended family. Family is what's best for children and is what they need. Community is important, of course. But to tell you the truth, when we go to Washington, DC, for the Eritrean festival, it's not the festival that's important. It's the house full of family. Who comes to the house, who sits together, who asks the children questions. That's the most important thing, to know that they are watching, and these people have high expectations of [my children]. Sometimes I think [my children] feel like they have too much pressure on them.

Looking back, what are you most proud of?

My children. I am very proud of my children. We got what we wanted. We planted seeds, and we got the product of what we wanted. I'm very happy to be their mother. No matter what, they come first. No matter what. And my husband knows that. I'm always there for them, always.

They're very lucky.

I'm lucky, too.

What was your favorite thing to eat growing up?

I was never a picky eater. I ate everything. My mother always said I was the blessed one in the family because I never complained about anything. Whatever she served, I always ate. Most of the time I loved to eat with the villagers. When they would come to the market to sell their stuff, they would spend the night in our house. So, when my mother served them food, I would sit with them and eat with them instead of [with] my dad and my siblings. I loved to eat with them because they had history.

Why did you choose to make shiro to share with us?

It's the most loved and appreciated dish by the Eritrean people. And it's easy. The hardest part is to make the [chickpea] powder. We bring it from Eritrea—we don't make it. The one we bring is ground chickpeas, garlic, onion, and spices. And they make it in bulk, and it lasts for like six months. I bring a lot when I come back from Eritrea, and I freeze it. It's vegan. And everyone loves to eat shiro. It's not spicy, it's not hot.

Would you say it bests represents Eritrean food?

Yes, yes. It's eaten in the villages because they can't afford to eat meat every day. In the city, people have money, and they go to the butcher and buy meat. In the villages, it's the main dish. Sometimes they don't use garlic or tomatoes, just the powder and oil. And salt. And still it tastes good. You can sprinkle the shiro powder instead of salt on injera [a flatbread made of ground teff], and it tastes good. I remember when I was a girl and went to church, my mother would put shiro on injera and fold it up and offer it to my grandmother and everyone who went to the church. My grandmother loved it. Shiro, especially now, people are improvising with it.

So, it's not used just as a cooked dish anymore?

Yes. They invite you to use it in a different way, even in Eritrea. Here, people say, "Why don't we use it as a soup?" And some people use cooked shiro as a spaghetti sauce. Shiro spaghetti!

What would you say is most misunderstood about Eritrea?

I just want people to know that Eritrea is the most peaceful country. People, we are very loving. And giving. We like to share, we like to give, we like to help people. We are very proud people. Eritreans are very proud people. We feel like there's no other country like Eritrea. Believe me. All of us. If something happens to Eritrea, we all unite. We don't let Eritrea fall down.

What do some call Eritrea?

The land of I Can Do It.

Kicha

(ERITREAN FLATBREADS)

These unleavened flatbreads are a great introduction to making bread at home, since the dough doesn't require any kneading or rising and you cook the breads quickly in a skillet—there's no oven involved. You can enjoy kicha warm, right out of the pan, as an accompaniment to any meal. For a full Ma Gehennet experience, serve the breads with her Zebhi Hamli (Stewed Spinach, page 44) and Shiro (Ground Chickpea Stew, page 45). You can use leftover kicha to make Kicha Fit Fit (page 43), a typical Eritrean breakfast of torn flatbreads mixed with butter, spices, and yogurt, or you can also make them specifically for that purpose. This recipe makes two large flatbreads that easily serve four, but feel free to use a small skillet to make smaller, individual flatbreads.

SERVES 4

1½ cups whole wheat flour

1 cup all-purpose flour

2 teaspoons kosher salt

1½ cups warm water

2 tablespoons canola oil

Place the whole wheat and all-purpose flours and salt in a large bowl and whisk well to combine. Using your hands, mix in the water. The batter will be like a very thick pancake batter.

Line a plate with paper towels and set aside. Set a 12-inch nonstick skillet over medium heat and add 1 tablespoon of the oil, tilting the pan so the oil lightly greases the bottom of the pan. Once the oil is hot, add half the dough to the skillet and use wet fingertips to gently and carefully press the dough into a wide circle that covers the surface of the skillet. Cover the skillet and cook until the top of the dough is glossy and the underside is golden brown, about 3 minutes. Carefully flip the bread over, cover, and cook until the second side is browned, another 2 to 3 minutes. Transfer the flatbread to the prepared plate, adding the remaining 1 tablespoon oil to the pan, and repeat the process with the remaining dough. Serve immediately while the breads are warm, or let cool to room temperature to use for Kicha Fit Fit. Leftover breads can be stored in a plastic bag at room temperature for a day and rewarmed in a skillet over low heat.

Kicha Fit Fit

(TORN FLATBREADS WITH SPICED BUTTER AND YOGURT)

Fit fit, broken pieces of flatbread cooked with fat and spices, is a typical dish throughout East Africa and is made with either Ethiopian-style injera (a flatbread made from fermented teff flour) or Eritrean kicha, like the one Ma Gehennet taught us how to make. It's a wonderful way to use up leftover flatbread of any kind. You could even use leftover pita bread. The drier the bread, the more it soaks up the spices and butter. Serve with plain yogurt dolloped on top. This is wonderful for breakfast or as a snack.

SERVES 4

3 tablespoons unsalted butter or ghee

1 tablespoon Berbere Spice Mix (page 50) or store-bought berbere

1 batch Kicha (Eritrean Flatbreads, page 40), torn into bite-size pieces (about 6 cups)

½ teaspoon kosher salt

1 cup plain yogurt

Place the butter in a large nonstick skillet set over medium heat. Once the butter melts, add the berbere and cook, stirring, until the spices sizzle and smell fragrant, about 30 seconds. Add the kicha pieces and sprinkle with the salt. Cook, stirring, until all the pieces of kicha are coated with the spiced butter and warmed through, about 3 minutes. Transfer the mixture to a serving platter or individual bowls, top with the yogurt, and serve immediately.

Zebhi Hamli

(STEWED SPINACH)

Ma Gehennet's simple stewed spinach is a wonderful, healthy side dish that can be served as part of a traditional Eritrean meal along with Ma Gehennet's Shiro (Ground Chickpea Stew, opposite) and Ma Gehennet's Kicha (Eritrean Flatbreads, page 40). It can also be served anywhere you would typically serve a cooked green—try it instead of creamed spinach with steak, under a grilled chicken breast or piece of fish, or with eggs in the morning. Toss it with cooked pasta and top with grated cheese. The dish is incredibly versatile and also can be made ahead—just cool it down, store it in an airtight container in the refrigerator for up to a few days, and rewarm in a heavy pot set over low heat (stirring as it heats) before serving.

SERVES 4

3 tablespoons canola oil

1 large red onion, finely chopped

2 garlic cloves, minced

1 chicken or vegetable bouillon cube

¼ cup tomato paste

½ cup water

Two 10-ounce packages frozen chopped spinach, thawed and drained

Kosher salt

2 jalapeños, stemmed and thinly sliced (use less or leave out if you don't want things too spicy)

Warm the oil in a large Dutch oven or heavy pot set over medium heat. Add the onion and garlic. Crumble the bouillon cube and sprinkle it over the onion. Cook, stirring occasionally, until just beginning to soften, about 5 minutes. Stir in the tomato paste and cook, stirring, until the mixture concentrates and is nearly dry, about 3 minutes. Add the water and stir to combine, then stir in the spinach. Sprinkle with a large pinch of salt, reduce the heat to low, cover, and cook, uncovering the pot every few minutes to stir and then re-covering it, until the spinach is very tender and all the aromatics have had a chance to flavor the spinach, about 10 minutes. Stir in the jalapeños and season the spinach to taste with salt. Serve immediately. Leftovers can be stored in an airtight container in the refrigerator for up to a few days and rewarmed in a heavy pot set over low heat (stir while you heat).

MA GEHENNET'S

Shiro

(GROUND CHICKPEA STEW)

A simple, nutritious, and completely vegan stew of ground chickpea flour and water, flavored with aromatics like onion, garlic, and chiles, shiro is one of the most, if not *the* most, popular dishes in Eritrea. According to Ma Gehennet, shiro is "the most favorite food in Eritrea. Children love it. Adults love it. We all love shiro." It's quick, affordable, and very filling. The recipe that follows is almost identical to Ma Gehennet's, except that we use plain chickpea flour (see page 18 for more about chickpea flour) and add Berbere Spice Mix. Ma Gehennet uses a shiro mix, which already has spices in it, that she brings back from Eritrea every two years and stores in her freezer (this mix is not easy to find in the United States). She also likes to make hers in a traditional clay pot known as a sali, because she says "food tastes better in a clay pot and it stays warm a long time." A regular Dutch oven or other heavy pot works well, too. Serve with Ma Gehennet's Kicha (Eritrean Flatbreads, page 40) and vegetables like Ma Gehennet's Zebhi Hamli (Stewed Spinach, opposite).

SERVES 4

1 large red onion, coarsely chopped

10 garlic cloves

½ cup canola oil

2 tablespoons Berbere Spice Mix (page 50) or store-bought berbere

Kosher salt

3 medium vine-ripened tomatoes, coarsely chopped

½ cup chickpea flour

2 cups water

2 jalapeños, stemmed and thinly sliced (use less or leave out if you don't want things too spicy)

Place the onion and garlic in a food processor and pulse until very finely ground. Set aside.

Warm the oil in a large Dutch oven or other heavy pot set over medium-low heat. Stir in the onion mixture, the berbere, and a large pinch of salt. Cover the pot and let the aromatics cook gently while you prepare the tomatoes.

Place the tomatoes in the food processor and pulse until they're finely ground. Add them to the onion mixture, increase the heat to high, and bring the mixture to a boil. Reduce the heat to low and stir in the chickpea flour. The mixture will be quite thick, like peanut butter. While stirring, slowly pour in the water to loosen the mixture. The mixture will be quite thick at first and not quite integrated, but keep stirring and adding the water in one slow steam until it becomes quite smooth. Bring the shiro to a boil, reduce the heat to low, and simmer for about 5 minutes to cook off the raw taste of the chickpea flour and integrate all the flavors. Stir in the jalapeños and season to taste with salt. Serve immediately. Leftovers can be stored in an airtight container in the refrigerator for up to a few days and rewarmed in a pot set over low heat (stir while you heat).

Shahan Ful

(MASHED LIMAS WITH ONIONS, TOMATOES, AND CHILES)

This completely vegan dish of mashed lima beans flavored with garlic, Berbere Spice Mix, and lemon juice can be served for breakfast, lunch, or dinner alongside some rice or as part of a larger spread of dishes for a big Eritrean meal. If you're not vegan, try it with a soft-boiled or fried egg on top. Shahan ful is very similar to ful medames, a staple Egyptian dish of mashed fava beans. For this recipe, we use frozen lima beans, making it incredibly quick to prepare and fresher tasting, since you don't have to soak and cook dried beans. If you want to cook this ahead of time, let it cool, refrigerate in an airtight container for up to a week, and rewarm gently in a saucepan over low heat (stirring as it heats) before serving.

SERVES 4

2 tablespoons canola oil

1 small yellow onion, finely chopped

2 garlic cloves, minced

½ jalapeño, stemmed and minced, plus additional, thinly sliced, for serving (use less or leave out if you don't want things too spicy)

1 tablespoon Berbere Spice Mix (page 50) or store-bought berbere

1 teaspoon kosher salt, plus more as needed

One 10-ounce package frozen lima beans, thawed

1 small tomato, finely diced

¼ cup water

2 tablespoons freshly squeezed lemon juice

Warm the oil in a medium saucepan set over medium heat. Add the onion, garlic, and minced jalapeño and cook, stirring occasionally, until just beginning to soften, about 3 minutes. Stir in the berbere and salt and cook, stirring, until very aromatic, about 1 minute. Add the lima beans, tomato, and water and stir well to combine with the aromatics. Reduce the heat to low, cover, and simmer until all of the flavors have a chance to get to know each other, about 10 minutes. Turn off the heat, stir in the lemon juice, and use a potato masher to crush the beans until they're the texture of mashed potatoes. Season the mixture to taste with salt and serve immediately, while hot, topped with the sliced jalapeños. Leftovers can be stored in an airtight container in the refrigerator for up to a few days and rewarmed in a heavy pot set over low heat (stir while you heat).

Firfir

(STEWED INJERA WITH MEAT, TOMATOES, AND ONIONS)

Very similar to the Kicha Fit Fit (Torn Flatbreads with Spiced Butter and Yogurt, page 43), this dish of torn bread mixed with a savory mixture of onions, beef, spices, and tomatoes gives new life to day-old bread and also stretches a little bit of meat to feed a lot of people. Ma Abeba calls for rosemary, which you don't see in any other recipe in this book, but its flavor complements the meat and tomatoes so well, bringing out the colonialist Italian influence that is so prevalent in East African cooking. The sour flavor of injera bread, made with teff flour that's slowly fermented like sourdough, adds a lot of dimension to this dish; injera can be purchased from any Ethiopian or Eritrean restaurant. It is also available in some African grocery stores. If you can't find it, feel free to make a batch of Kicha (Eritrean Flatbreads) and use it in place of injera. You won't have the same exact sour flavor, but it will still be very tasty. You could also use leftover sourdough bread, torn into cubes, almost like an Eritrean panzanella (an Italian bread salad).

SERVES 4

2 large tomatoes

3 tablespoons canola oil

1 large yellow onion, finely chopped

½ teaspoon kosher salt, plus more as needed

2 garlic cloves, minced

One 2-inch piece ginger, peeled and minced

Leaves from one 6-inch sprig of rosemary, minced

1 tablespoon Berbere Spice Mix (page 50) or store-bought berbere

2 tablespoons tomato paste

1 cup water

½ pound boneless beef chuck or other stew meat, cut into ½-inch pieces

1 large piece store-bought injera, or 1 recipe Kicha (Eritrean Flatbreads, page 40), torn into bite-sized pieces (about 6 cups total)

1 jalapeño, stemmed and thinly sliced, for serving (use less or leave out if you don't want things too spicy)

Cut off and discard a thin slice from the stem end of each tomato and then coarsely grate the tomatoes on a box grater directly into a bowl. Discard the skins. Set aside.

Warm the oil in a large Dutch oven or other heavy pot set over medium heat. Stir in the onion, sprinkle with the salt, and cook, stirring, until softened, about 10 minutes. Add the garlic, ginger, rosemary, berbere, and tomato paste and cook, stirring occasionally, until everything smells wonderfully fragrant, about 1 minute. Add the tomatoes and cook until they've nearly evaporated, about 5 minutes (this will help concentrate their flavor). Add the water and meat, reduce the heat to low, cover the pot, and cook until the meat is very tender, about 20 minutes. Stir in the injera and cook, stirring gently, until the bread absorbs all of the liquid, about 2 minutes. Season the firfir to taste with salt. Transfer to a serving platter, top with the jalapeño, and serve immediately. Leftovers can be stored in an airtight container in the refrigerator for a couple of days.

Berbere Spice Mix

Berbere is *the* spice mix of Ethiopia and Eritrea. It's centered on dried chiles, both spicy ones and sweet paprika, and spices like fenugreek and coriander seeds. The mix we use also features warm flavors including cardamom, allspice, cinnamon, and ginger. It's at once spicy and a tiny bit sweet and full of layers. Like Xawaash Spice Mix (page 74) in Somalia and dry rubs for barbecue in the American South, berbere differs from region to region, family to family, even neighbor to neighbor. Which is to say, feel free to add a little bit more of one spice or less of another if you'd like, or try swapping one for something else. Try it in Ma Gehennet's Shiro (Ground Chickpea Stew, page 45), Doro Wat (Stewed Chicken Legs with Berbere and Eggs, page 53), or Shahan Ful (Mashed Limas with Onions, Tomatoes, and Chiles, page 47). You can also add it to any stew or braise (start with about 1 tablespoon berbere for every four servings) or try rubbing a light coating on shrimp or chicken thighs before grilling (you can let them sit overnight in the refrigerator after seasoning or just season right before grilling).

MAKES ABOUT ⅔ CUP

One 1-inch piece cinnamon stick

1 tablespoon coriander seeds

1 teaspoon fenugreek seeds

1 teaspoon black peppercorns

6 cardamom pods

3 allspice berries

4 dried chiles de árbol, stemmed and seeded

¼ cup dried onion flakes

3 tablespoons sweet paprika

½ teaspoon ground ginger

½ teaspoon freshly grated nutmeg

Place the cinnamon, coriander, fenugreek, peppercorns, cardamom, and allspice in a small heavy skillet set over medium heat. Cook, stirring constantly, until the smell is very aromatic and the spices are lightly toasted, about 2 minutes. Let cool. Transfer the mixture to a clean coffee grinder, add the chiles and onion flakes, and grind to a fine powder (or use a mortar and pestle and some elbow grease). Transfer the ground spices to a fine-mesh sieve set over a bowl and sift. Regrind whatever large pieces remain in the sieve and add them to the bowl with the ground spices. Add the paprika, ginger, and nutmeg. Whisk well to combine and transfer the mixture to an airtight jar. Store in a cool, dark place for up to 3 months.

Doro Wat

(STEWED CHICKEN LEGS WITH BERBERE AND EGGS)

This stew is a testament to the benefit of having Berbere Spice Mix in your cupboard—it takes a simple braised chicken that you can make any night of the week from basic to really special. Serve with cooked rice or flatbread such as Ma Gehennet's Kicha (Eritrean Flatbreads, page 40).

SERVES 4 TO 6

3 tablespoons unsalted butter or ghee

2 large red onions, finely diced

6 garlic cloves, minced

2 tablespoons minced ginger

3 tablespoons Berbere Spice Mix (page 50) or store-bought berbere

1 teaspoon kosher salt, plus more as needed

2 medium vine-ripened tomatoes, finely diced

1 cup water

8 chicken drumsticks

6 large eggs, hard-boiled and peeled

Melt the butter in a medium saucepan set over medium heat. Add the onion, garlic, and ginger and cook, stirring occasionally, until just beginning to soften, about 5 minutes. Stir in the berbere and salt and cook, stirring, until very aromatic, about 1 minute. Add the tomatoes and cook, stirring until they've reduced down and the mixture is almost dry, about 10 minutes. Add the water, increase the heat to high, and bring to a boil. Lower the heat to maintain a simmer. Season the chicken pieces all over with salt and then nestle them into the pot. Cover and cook, uncovering the pot every so often to stir, until the chicken is very tender, about 1 hour. Add the eggs and cook, stirring every so often, until the eggs are heated through and nicely coated with the sauce, about 10 minutes.

Use a slotted spoon to transfer the chicken legs and eggs to a serving dish. Increase the heat to high, return the sauce to a boil, and cook until slightly reduced and thickened, about 5 minutes. Spoon the sauce over the chicken and eggs. Serve immediately. Leftovers can be stored in an airtight container in the refrigerator for up to a few days and rewarmed in a heavy pot set over low heat (stir while you heat).

Buna

(ERITREAN COFFEE)

Ma Gehennet prepared traditional Eritrean coffee at her home for us. The process, a coffee ceremony, is a central part of Eritrean daily life. One of the most beautiful parts of the ritual is that it's meant to be shared—coffee is a means of gathering people in a home. To make this coffee the truly traditional way, get yourself a jebena, a traditional Eritrean clay coffeepot with a spherical base, a small handle, a narrow spout, and a circular holder in which to place the pot after the coffee is brewed (we've seen some beautiful jebenas on eBay and Etsy). Whether or not you roast your own coffee beans at home, grind them with ginger, and brew them in a traditional jebena as described in the recipe that follows, consider a pot of coffee an invitation to spend time being present together with your family and neighbors. Ma Gehennet likes to serve her coffee with freshly popped popcorn for snacking on. The sound (and fragrance!) of the beans roasting and the corn kernels popping at the same time is beautiful music. It's also traditional to have incense burning during the coffee ceremony; this adds to the overall aromatic atmosphere. The repeated brewing gets the most out of the coffee beans, and most important, prolongs the coffee ceremony, which, of course, means you spend more time together.

SERVES 4

¾ cup green coffee beans (see page 20 for more information)

Three 1-inch pieces dried ginger

3 cups cold water

Granulated sugar, for serving

Place the coffee beans in a small heavy pot set over high heat. Cook the beans, shaking and swirling the pot continuously, until the beans become very dark and begin to smoke, about 5 minutes. Be sure to waft the smoke around the room for everyone to smell—this is part of the ceremony.

Once the beans are black all over, pour them onto a woven straw mat (or a sheet pan lined with parchment paper) to cool slightly and then bend the mat and funnel the beans into an electric coffee grinder. Add the ginger and grind the coffee and ginger together until finely ground. Pour the ground coffee back onto the mat, fold it, and use it to funnel the grounds into a jebena. Fill the jebena with the water and set over high heat. When the water begins to boil and you can see steam coming from the top of the jebena, pour the coffee into a small pot with a spout or a pitcher and then pour it back into the jebena (this will help to cool it

momentarily so that it doesn't boil over). Set the jebena on its traditional circular holder and plug the top with its filter (traditionally made of horsehair), which will keep the coffee grounds from ending up in your cups. Let the jebena sit for a few minutes while you get your coffee cups ready on a tray (this is essential to catch drips of the coffee when you pour it). Put a spoonful of sugar in the bottom of each coffee cup, if your guests take their coffee sweet. Pour the coffee for all of your guests until all the cups are full, without stopping the pouring in between cups (here's where the tray comes in very handy). It's okay that some of the coffee drips—this is preferable to having the coffee grounds get remixed with the brewed coffee each time you tilt the jebena to pour.

Traditionally, the coffee grounds are brewed and served up to three more times for a total of four brews (and, yes, you are to drink each round!). The first round is called awel, the second kale'i, the third bereka, and the fourth dereja, which is not always poured, but typically is if elders are present.

Chapter Two

Somal

ia

People have lived in Somalia since the Paleolithic era and, thanks to its coastline (the longest on the African continent), it has been a perpetual center of commerce. It was part of what the ancient Egyptians called the Land of Punt, and many empires traded throughout the area in the Middle Ages.

Luigi Robecchi Bricchetti, an Italian explorer, is said to have named Somalia. His travels, the first extensive travels of any European in the area, heralded more. During the late 1800s, England and Italy both established colonies in the area, known as British Somaliland and Italian Somaliland.

For the first twenty years of the 1900s, the Somali Dervish movement, led by Mohammed Abdullah Hassan, provided armed resistance from the inside and attempted to remove the colonial forces. Ultimately, Italy proved the more powerful and took control of nearly the entire area in 1920. In 1960, the Somali Republic, ruled by a civilian government, was formed, and in 1969, the Somali Democratic Republic was officially established, but collapsed in 1991 when the Somali civil war started.

During the beginning of the 2000s, a series of interim solutions began, starting with the Transitional National Government in 2000, then the Transitional Federal Government just four years later. A provisional constitution was passed in August 2012, returning Somalia to a federation, and the Federal Government of Somalia was formed.

Geography and Climate

Part of the Horn of Africa, Somalia sits east of Ethiopia, west of the Somali Sea and the Guardafui Channel, and south of the Gulf of Aden. Djibouti is to Somalia's northwest and Kenya to its southeast. Of all the countries on the entire African continent, Somalia has the longest coastline. It's located at the mouth of the Bab el-Mandeb, the entry point to the Red Sea and the Suez Canal. Since Somalia is located at the tip of the Horn of Africa, you could say it *is* the horn. It's hot year-round, and rainfall is irregular. Mogadishu, Somalia's capital city, is home to over two million residents. Hargeisa, its second largest city, has a population just over a million people.

Economy and Resources

Somalia's economy is an informal one, based mostly on livestock, money transfer companies, and communications. Its biggest exports include bananas, fish, and charcoal. Somalia is one of the world's major suppliers of frankincense and myrrh. Other valuable agricultural items include sorghum, sugar, and corn, but these mostly stay within the country. Somalia also holds a number of different natural resources, including copper, gypsum, and natural gas.

People

Somalia's estimated population is about fourteen million people, and about 85 percent of its residents are ethnic Somalis, making the country one of the most culturally homogeneous in Africa. Ethnic minorities (these include Bantus, Yemenis, Indians, Italians, and Persians) mostly live in the southern regions of the country.

Language

The official languages of Somalia are Somali and Arabic.

Religion

The majority of Somalis are Sunni Muslim, which is the largest denomination of Islam. Almost all food in Somalia is halal, which means there's no pork, and no alcohol is consumed.

Ma Halima

HOME
Minneapolis, Minnesota

HER RECIPES
Sabaayad (Somali Flatbreads, page 76)
Beef Suqaar (page 84)

Why did you choose to make sabaayad to share with us?
I love to eat it. It's a good food.

What do you think of when you make it?
I remember my mom. She taught me.

What dish do you think best represents Somalian food?
Meat and milk. Bariis [rice]. Hilib ari [goat meat]. Sheep meat. Camel meat. Cow meat. We love meat and rice.

What would you say is most misunderstood about Somalia?
Somalia is beautiful. People don't know that, but I was there. Somalia is the best country to live, but we misunderstand because of the war. My dream is to go back to Somalia and build a house and live there. I love Somalia. It's a beautiful place.

Do your children and grandchildren know how to cook?
My children do, yes. They know.

Did you teach them how to cook?
Yes.

What does passing on food traditions mean to you?

I have different cultures. I was born in Ethiopia, raised in Somalia, and grew up in Saudi Arabia, and now I live here. So, for every country, I have different favorites. From Saudi Arabia, I like to eat haneeth [a mixture of rice, lamb, and spices]. From Ethiopia, I like to eat injera. From Somalia, I like to eat bariis and spaghetti and goat meat. I am a mixed person. I cannot say only one country.

What does home mean to you?

Very big deal. I love home.

Looking back, what are you most proud of?

When my daughter graduated, and she threw her cap and gown. And the day I married my husband.

What was your favorite thing to eat growing up?

Ha, who knows! Maybe sheep meat.

Who made it?

Me! I made it.

Has your cooking changed now that you live in America?

No, it's the same. Maybe the spices are different. But I can always order spices from back home, and I can cook.

How has the process of finding ingredients here changed?

You can find whatever you want now. But when we came in 1993, there was no store. Now, everywhere, there's a store.

Why is it important to cook food from home?

Because it's not junk food!

Minneapolis, Minnesota

Ma Sahra

HOME
Eastleigh, Kenya (also known
as Nairobi's Little Mogadishu);
originally from Wajir, which used
to be part of Somalia but is now part
of Kenya

HER RECIPE
Spiced Chicken and Onion Samosas (page 88)

When do you make samosas?

When you have good visitors, or really whenever you like.

What kind of samosas do you make?

Today, I made chicken, but you can do meat samosas or vegetable samosas. Whatever type. Any kind of samosa.

What dish do you think best represents Somali food?

Almost everything, because Somalis live everywhere. But the most special is rice and chapattis [flatbreads].

What would you say is most misunderstood about Somalia?

They think we are bad people, that we are proud, that we don't talk to other people. But look at us. Within a few minutes of talking, I take you as my daughter.

Do you enjoy cooking?

I do! If I was told to cook a big meal in four hours, I could do it.

What do you most enjoy cooking?

Rice and chapattis. I'm very proud because I can cook every food and I love every food. If you are a visitor and say you don't eat something, that's not me.

Did you teach your children how to cook?

Yes. I remember once it was Ramadan, and we had visitors and had to cook for so many people. My daughter just started at it, *chop chop chop*, and I just couldn't believe it.

What does passing on food traditions mean to you?

I'm proud to pass them on. Being a Somali mother, if there is a party or whatever, I'm called to cook and I'm proud. I'll make samosas or whatever, whatever.

What was your favorite thing to eat growing up?
Mchele [rice]. And chapatti, injera, and soft drinks!

And who cooked the mchele?
Me, of course, me.

But when you were younger—who cooked it?
Oh, my mother. My mom. I'm so happy she brought me up and taught me how to make it, and now I can teach all of you.

What does being a woman mean in the Somali community?
It is good. Like me, I'm a grandmother. When we sit together like this, I'll tell you everything. Whether it's a story or it's cooking. We pass time.

Digaag Qumbe

(CHICKEN STEW WITH YOGURT AND COCONUT)

Made with bite-sized pieces of boneless, skinless chicken thighs, this stew is also incredibly quick cooking. Serve over cooked rice or on a bed of spinach—this is Hawa's preference (something she mentioned when she got to share this recipe with *Bon Appétit*). Either way, serve it with bananas alongside for the most authentic Somali experience. The combination is not well known in the United States, but you can help it become known—it's great.

SERVES 4

2 medium vine-ripened tomatoes, coarsely chopped

1 jalapeño, stemmed and coarsely chopped (use less or leave out if you don't want things too spicy)

1 red bell pepper, stemmed, seeded, and coarsely chopped

1 tablespoon tomato paste

½ cup plain yogurt

2 tablespoons Xawaash Spice Mix (page 74)

2 teaspoons kosher salt, plus more as needed

¼ cup extra-virgin olive oil or canola oil

1 large red onion, finely chopped

2 large garlic cloves, minced

1 tablespoon minced ginger

1 baking potato, cut into bite-sized pieces

2 carrots, cut into thin coins

1 pound boneless, skinless chicken thighs, cut into bite-sized pieces

1 cup full-fat unsweetened coconut milk

Large handful of cilantro leaves, finely chopped

Cooked rice and bananas, for serving

In the jar of a blender, combine the tomatoes, jalapeño, bell pepper, tomato paste, yogurt, xawaash, and salt and puree until smooth. Set aside.

Warm the oil in a large Dutch oven or other heavy pot set over medium heat. Add the onion, garlic, and ginger and cook, stirring occasionally, until just beginning to soften, about 5 minutes. Stir in the blended tomato mixture, bring the mixture to a boil, then immediately lower the heat, cover, and cook until very fragrant, about 10 minutes. This initial cooking forms the base of the sauce. Stir in the potato, carrots, chicken, and coconut milk. Cover the pot and cook, uncovering it to stir occasionally, until the vegetables are tender and the chicken is cooked through, about 30 minutes. Season the stew to taste with salt. Serve hot, sprinkled with the cilantro, over cooked rice, and with bananas alongside (don't slice the bananas, just serve them whole and take a bite as you eat the stew). Leftovers can be stored in an airtight container in the refrigerator for up to a few days and rewarmed in a heavy pot set over low heat (stir while you heat).

Xawaash Spice Mix

Xawaash (pronounced *HA-wash*) comes from the Arabic word hawaij, which is used to describe Yemeni spice blends. Xawaash touches just about every Somali dish. It's like the garam masala of Somalia, and the mix of flavors is truly the flavor of the Indian Ocean. Each Somali home cook prepares hers differently. This is how Hawa prepares hers. She always makes a large batch so she has it on hand to add to dishes as she cooks, adding layers of deep, warm flavors to everything from Digaag Qumbe (Chicken Stew with Yogurt and Coconut, page 73) to Bariis (Basmati Rice Pilaf with Raisins, page 87), Suugo Suqaar (Pasta Sauce with Beef, page 90), and Somali Beef Stew (page 93). You can also toss it on vegetables or chicken before roasting or use it as a dry rub on any type of meat before grilling.

MAKES ABOUT 1¼ CUPS

One 2-inch piece cinnamon stick

½ cup cumin seeds

½ cup coriander seeds

2 tablespoons black peppercorns

6 cardamom pods

1 teaspoon whole cloves

2 tablespoons ground turmeric

Place the cinnamon stick in a small zip-top plastic bag, seal it, and bang it a couple of times with a rolling pin, skillet, or mallet (anything firm and heavy) to break it into small pieces.

Place the cinnamon pieces, cumin, coriander, peppercorns, cardamom, and cloves in a small heavy skillet set over medium heat. Cook, stirring constantly, until the smell is very aromatic and the spices are lightly toasted, about 2 minutes. Let cool. Transfer the mixture to a clean coffee grinder and grind into a fine powder (or use a mortar and pestle and some elbow grease). Transfer the ground spices to a fine-mesh sieve set over a bowl and sift. Regrind whatever large pieces remain in the sieve and add them to the bowl with the ground spices. Add the turmeric. Whisk well to combine and transfer the mixture to an airtight jar. Store in a cool, dark place for up to 6 months.

Sabaayad

(SOMALI FLATBREADS)

Ma Halima suggests serving these flatbreads with any type of stew or cooked meat, such as her Beef Suqaar (page 84), a sauté of beef and onions. She makes her sabaayad quite large and in huge quantities, since she makes them at the restaurant where she works, but we scaled the recipe down to manageable pieces that can be cooked and flipped easily. Folding the dough repeatedly with oil makes them like a laminated pastry with distinct layers that flake apart when you eat them (um . . . yum). You can make them up to 3 days ahead and refrigerate. Before serving, wrap them in aluminum foil and warm in a 250°F oven for just a few minutes, or reheat in a dry skillet.

MAKES 8 FLATBREADS

3 cups all-purpose flour, plus more for rolling out the dough

1 cup whole wheat flour

1 teaspoon baking powder

2 tablespoons granulated sugar

1 teaspoon kosher salt

1½ cups whole milk

Large handful of cilantro leaves, chopped

4 tablespoons canola oil, plus more as needed

Place the all-purpose flour, whole wheat flour, baking powder, sugar, and salt in a large bowl and whisk together. Warm the milk in a saucepan set over medium heat (or in the microwave) until small bubbles appear around the edges, about 2 minutes. Add the milk, cilantro, and 2 tablespoons of the oil to the flour mixture and stir with a wooden spoon until a shaggy dough forms (this might take a couple of minutes). If the dough is too dry to come together, add warm water a tablespoonful at a time, until it comes together (alternatively, if the dough is too wet, add more all-purpose flour a tablespoonful at a time until it comes together).

Sprinkle a clean work surface lightly with flour. Transfer the dough to it and knead, pushing the dough away from you and pulling it back quickly, until it is quite elastic and springy. It will take a solid 10 to 15 minutes of kneading (you can also knead for 5 minutes in a stand mixer fitted with the dough hook if you prefer).

Use your hand to coat a clean large bowl with 2 tablespoons of the oil and transfer the dough to it, turning the dough to coat with the oil. Cover the bowl with a clean kitchen towel or plastic wrap and let it sit in a warm spot in your kitchen (the inside of a microwave or an oven—neither of which

should be turned on—is a good bet) until the dough is a bit puffy and soft, about 45 minutes.

Transfer the dough to a flour-sprinkled work surface and cut it into eight equal pieces. Working with one piece of dough at a time, use a rolling pin to roll the dough into a ¼-inch-thick oval measuring about 8 inches long at its widest point. Use a clean pastry brush or your hands to brush a thin layer of oil (about 1 teaspoon) on the surface of the dough and then fold it in half, brush with a little bit more oil (about 1 teaspoon), and fold it in half one more time. Use your rolling pin to flatten the dough one final time into a ¼-inch-thick oval measuring about 8 inches long at its widest point. Repeat the process with the remaining pieces of dough.

Line a serving basket or dish with a cloth napkin and set aside. Set a large cast-iron skillet or other heavy skillet over medium heat and let it warm up for 2 minutes. Place one sabaayad in the skillet and cook until bubbles start to form on the surface and the underside is brown, about 2 minutes. Flip the sabaayad, reduce the heat to low, and, using a spatula, press the sabaayad down in the skillet to make sure all of the edges are in contact with the skillet, then cook until the second side is golden brown, about 2 more minutes. Transfer the sabaayad to the prepared serving basket or dish, cover with another napkin, and repeat the process with the remaining pieces of dough. Serve warm. Leftover breads can be stored in a plastic bag at room temperature for a day and rewarmed in a skillet set over low heat before serving.

Somali Cilantro and Green Chile Pepper Sauce

Hawa's company, Basbaas, is named for the Somali term for chile pepper, and her ready-made sauces are just like this one—an everyday condiment that makes everything it touches better. In fact, this cilantro and green chile pepper sauce that delivers spice and acid in big doses is a version of Basbaas's green sauce. Serve it on . . . anything. From scrambled eggs to grilled fish, tacos to roast chicken, a bowl of rice to a grilled steak, it's one of the most versatile recipes in the book.

MAKES ABOUT 1 CUP

½ cup full-fat unsweetened coconut milk

3 tablespoons freshly squeezed lime juice, plus more as needed

2 tablespoons white vinegar or white wine vinegar

½ cup packed cilantro leaves

2 jalapeños, stemmed and coarsely chopped

2 large garlic cloves, minced

2 teaspoons granulated sugar

1 teaspoon kosher salt, plus more as needed

In the jar of a blender or in a food processor, combine the coconut milk, lime juice, vinegar, cilantro, jalapeños, garlic, sugar, and salt and puree until smooth. Season the sauce to taste with more lime juice or salt if needed. Serve immediately or place in a jar and store in the refrigerator for up to a week.

Canjeero

(SOURDOUGH PANCAKES)

Canjeero, sometimes also called lahoh, are thin pancakes made from a fermented batter. They are similar to Ethiopian injera but lighter in flavor, smaller, and faster and easier to make. The pancakes are typically enjoyed for breakfast. You can spread canjeero with a little butter, ghee, or sesame oil and sprinkle with sugar, if you'd like. Serve with hot tea or, for a special treat, alongside cups of Shaah Cadays (Somali Spiced Tea with Milk, page 94). You can also serve canjeero with savory foods in the morning or alongside lunch or dinner. They're also great for scooping up stewed meats like Somali Beef Stew (page 93).

MAKES 12 PANCAKES

1 cup finely ground white cornmeal (see page 18)

1 teaspoon active dry yeast

5 cups warm water

3 tablespoons granulated sugar

2 teaspoons baking powder

1 teaspoon kosher salt

4 cups all-purpose flour

1 teaspoon unsalted butter or canola oil

Place the cornmeal, yeast, and 2 cups of the water in a large bowl and stir together vigorously with a spoon. Cover the bowl with a clean kitchen towel or plastic wrap and let it sit at room temperature until small bubbles appear on top and the mixture has risen slightly, about 1 hour.

Add the remaining 3 cups water, the sugar, baking powder, and salt to the bowl and stir well to combine. Whisk in the flour until the mixture is smooth. Cover the bowl with the kitchen towel and let it sit at room temperature for at least 4 hours and up to 24 hours; the longer it sits, the more flavor it will develop. The mixture will have some bubbles on the surface.

When you're ready to cook the pancakes, place the butter in a large nonstick skillet over medium heat. Once the butter has melted and the skillet is hot, stir the batter well and ladle enough into the skillet to form a thin, even layer across the bottom, tilting the pan to coat the surface (the exact amount will depend on the size of your skillet but figure about ½ cup). Use the rounded base of your ladle to swirl batter to make some circular grooves on the surface. Cover the skillet with a lid and cook until no liquid remains on the surface and the underside is barely golden brown, about 2 minutes. Transfer the pancake to a plate and repeat with the remaining batter (no need to add more butter after the first pancake). Stack the pancakes as you make them and serve them warm as they are or rolled up as in the photo.

Beef Suqaar

Roughly translated from Arabic, *suqaar* means "small ones" and the dish is basically a quickly cooked mixture of small pieces of meat and vegetables. Think of this as a Somali stir-fry. Suqaar is a very flexible dish and can be made with any type of meat. Goat is the most traditional, but here we opt for beef. Serve it just as Ma Halima does, with cooked rice or Bariis (Basmati Rice Pilaf with Raisins, page 87), chopped lettuce, and big pieces of lemon to squeeze on top of everything.

SERVES 4

2 tablespoons canola oil

1½ pounds boneless beef chuck or other stew meat, cut into bite-sized pieces

1 large yellow onion, coarsely chopped

Kosher salt

2 large carrots, thinly sliced

1 tablespoon ground cumin

1 tablespoon ground turmeric

¼ cup water

1 small green bell pepper, stemmed, seeded, and thinly sliced

2 tablespoons freshly squeezed lime juice

Large handful of cilantro leaves, coarsely chopped

Warm the oil in a large Dutch oven or other heavy pot set over medium-high heat. Add the beef and onion and sprinkle with a large pinch of salt. Cook, stirring occasionally, until the beef is browned in spots and the onion is beginning to become tender, about 10 minutes. Add the carrots and sprinkle the cumin and turmeric over everything, along with another large pinch of salt. Stir in the water, cover, and cook until the carrots are beginning to get tender, about 5 minutes. Stir in the bell pepper, cover the skillet again, and cook until the carrots and peppers are just barely tender, about 5 minutes. Turn off the heat, stir in the lime juice, and season to taste with salt. Sprinkle with the cilantro and serve immediately. Leftovers can be stored in an airtight container in the refrigerator for up to a few days and rewarmed in a skillet set over low heat (stir while you heat).

Bariis

(BASMATI RICE PILAF WITH RAISINS)

Bariis is a rice pilaf that Somalis often serve with cooked meat like Somali Beef Stew (page 93) or stewed chicken. The mix of savory and sweet, more specifically the combination of cooked onions, warm spices, and sweet raisins, is very typical of Somali food. Bariis even makes for a wonderful breakfast with a fried or soft-boiled egg on top. Rinsing and soaking the rice ahead of time really helps the grains let go of their dusty coating and also cook more quickly and evenly. A pot of bariis helps Hawa feel at home and connected to her Somali family and roots even when she is very far away from both of those.

SERVES 4

1 cup basmati rice

2 tablespoons extra-virgin olive oil or canola oil

1 small red onion, thinly sliced into half-moons

One 2-inch piece cinnamon stick

2 whole cloves

2 garlic cloves, minced

Pinch of ground cardamom

1 small tomato, finely chopped

Kosher salt

3 tablespoons golden raisins or regular raisins

1 tablespoon Xawaash Spice Mix (page 74)

1½ cups boiling water

Place the rice in a fine-mesh sieve and rinse with cold tap water, stirring the rice gently with your hands, until the water runs clear. Place the rinsed rice in a bowl, cover with cold water, and let it soak for at least 10 minutes and up to 30 minutes.

Warm the oil in a medium saucepan set over medium heat. Once the oil is hot, add the onion and cook, stirring, until it begins to soften, about 5 minutes. Add the cinnamon and cloves and cook, stirring, until the mixture smells very fragrant, about 5 minutes. Stir in the garlic and cardamom and cook, stirring, until they're also quite fragrant, about 30 seconds. Add the tomato and a large pinch of salt, then increase the heat to high. Cook, stirring, until the juice from the tomato has evaporated and the mixture is like a thick paste, about 2 minutes. Drain the rice and add it to the pot, along with another large pinch of salt. Reduce the heat to low, cover, and cook, stirring, until the mixture is quite dry and the rice smells nutty and is opaque, about 5 minutes. Stir in the raisins, spice mix, and boiling water. Reduce the heat to low, cover, and cook until the rice has absorbed the liquid and is tender, about 15 minutes. Turn off the heat and let the rice sit, covered, for at least 10 minutes before fluffing with a spoon or fork. If you can find the cinnamon stick and cloves, fish them out and discard them (otherwise, just warn your guests to avoid eating these). Serve the rice immediately, while hot. Leftovers can be stored in an air-tight container in the refrigerator and rewarmed in a 300°F oven or in a skillet over low heat.

Spiced Chicken and Onion Samosas

"Don't be in a hurry," Ma Sahra says about cooking samosas, the crispy fried triangular pastries that can be filled with anything from spiced chicken and onions (like these) to every kind of vegetable, goat meat, or even fish. Anything can be a samosa! Samosas are also found in Indian cooking, and it's no surprise that they found their way across the Indian Ocean to Somalia and neighboring countries. They're sometimes called sambusas, and in Mozambique, you'll find them referred to as chamussas (Mozambique is home to one of the largest Indian populations in Africa, because the Indian state of Goa and Mozambique were once part of the Portuguese empire).

MAKES 8 SAMOSAS

1 cup all-purpose flour, plus more for dusting

⅓ cup warm water

3 tablespoons canola oil, plus more for frying

Kosher salt

1 large baking potato, coarsely chopped

1 small yellow onion, finely diced

1 small red bell pepper, stemmed, seeded, and finely diced

2 garlic cloves, minced

1 tablespoon Xawaash Spice Mix (page 74)

½ pound boneless, skinless chicken thighs, finely chopped

Put the flour, water, 1 tablespoon of the oil, and a large pinch of salt in a large bowl and stir with a wooden spoon until a dough forms. Transfer the dough to a lightly floured work surface and knead until it is smooth, elastic, soft, and doesn't stick to your fingers, about 5 minutes. Return the dough to the bowl you mixed it in, lightly dust the dough with flour, and cover with a clean kitchen towel or plastic wrap. Set it aside to rest until soft and slightly risen, about 30 minutes.

While the dough rests, place the potato and a large pinch of salt in a small saucepan and cover with cold water. Set the saucepan over high heat and bring the water to a boil. Lower the heat to maintain a simmer and cook until the potato is tender, about 15 minutes, then drain and set aside.

Meanwhile, warm the remaining 2 tablespoons oil in a large skillet set over medium heat. Add the onion, bell pepper, garlic, and Xawaash. Cook, stirring occasionally, until the onion begins to soften, about 5 minutes. Add the chicken and sprinkle with a large pinch of salt. Cook, stirring occasionally, until the chicken is cooked through, about 10 minutes. Turn off the heat and stir in the potato. The whole mixture should be like a rough mash. Let the filling cool to room temperature, then season it to taste with salt.

Transfer the dough to a lightly floured work surface and divide it in half. Use a floured rolling pin to roll each piece into a thin 12-inch square (or as close to a square as you can get). If the dough resists as you're rolling it, just let it rest for a few minutes before proceeding.

Cut each square into four even strips. Divide the filling among the strips, placing it in a mound at one end of each strip, about 1 inch from the edge. Working with one strip at a time, fold the outer inch of the dough up and over the filling to form a triangle. Take the outer end and fold it down to add another layer of dough onto the triangle. Continue folding up and down in a zigzag to continue encasing the filling in more layers of dough until you reach the end of the strip. Repeat the entire process with the remaining dough and filling. You will have eight triangles by the time you're done.

Line a plate or tray with paper towels and set aside. Heat 1 inch of oil in a Dutch oven or other heavy pot set over medium-high heat until it reaches 375°F on an instant-read thermometer or until the edge of a samosa dipped into the oil sizzles on contact. Fry the samosas, in batches if necessary, depending on the size of your pot, until they are browned on all sides, about 5 minutes per samosa. It's better to fry in batches rather than crowding the pot. Note that as you add the cold samosas to the hot oil, the oil temperature will drop, so you might have to adjust your heat as you fry. Home frying is a bit of a dance of adjusting the temperature and being patient while things brown evenly. Trust your instincts! Transfer the browned samosas to the prepared plate or tray to drain. Serve immediately, while they're hot (but truthfully, they're good at room temperature, too). Leftovers can be stored in an airtight container in the refrigerator for up to a few days and rewarmed on a baking sheet, uncovered, in a 350°F oven for about 10 minutes before serving.

Suugo Suqaar

(PASTA SAUCE WITH BEEF)

Italy's colonization of southern Somalia during the nineteenth and twentieth centuries had a lasting impact on Somali cuisine. Pasta is just as popular as Canjeero (Sourdough Pancakes, page 83). Suugo is the most popular of Somali pasta sauces and resembles an easy weeknight meat sauce but the added flavor of Xawaash Spice Mix makes it distinctly Somali (and distinctly tasty). You can substitute ground turkey or ground chicken in place of the beef if you'd like. Serve with cooked pasta (any shape will work, whether it be a strandlike spaghetti or a shorter cut like penne). If you're gluten-free, try serving it over Ma Maria's Xima (Smooth Cornmeal Porridge, page 182) or roasted sweet potatoes instead of pasta.

SERVES 4

3 tablespoons extra-virgin olive oil or canola oil

2 garlic cloves, minced

1 small green bell pepper, stemmed, seeded, and finely chopped

1 small red onion, finely chopped

1 pound ground beef

3 tablespoons Xawaash Spice Mix (page 74)

1 teaspoon kosher salt, plus more as needed

2 tablespoons tomato paste

One 28-ounce can diced tomatoes, with their juices

Cooked spaghetti (or whatever shape pasta you like) and coarsely chopped cilantro, for serving

Place the oil in a large skillet set over medium-high heat. Once the oil is hot, add the garlic, bell pepper, and onion. Cook, stirring occasionally, until the vegetables begin to soften, about 8 minutes. Add the beef, Xawaash, and salt and cook, stirring occasionally to break up the beef, until the meat is browned, about 15 minutes.

Add the tomato paste and diced tomatoes (and their juices). Fill the tomato can halfway with water and add it to the pot. Stir well to combine, being sure to scrape up any bits stuck to the bottom of the skillet. Increase the heat to high and bring the sauce to a boil, then decrease the heat to low and simmer, stirring occasionally as the sauce cooks, for 30 minutes. Season the sauce to taste with salt. Serve hot over cooked spaghetti, with the cilantro sprinkled on top. Leftovers can be stored in an airtight container in the refrigerator for up to a few days and rewarmed in a heavy pot set over low heat (stir while you heat).

Somali Beef Stew

This stew is a wonderful way to stretch a little meat into a large, satisfying pot of food. The combination of Xawaash Spice Mix and tomato paste is particularly great, a match made in flavor heaven. Serve over plain rice with hot sauce and cilantro for topping, lime wedges for squeezing over, and bananas for eating alongside (this is very typical in Somalia—a bite of stew and rice followed by a bite of banana and so on). You can make the stew up to a week in advance and refrigerate it in an airtight container (it gets even better the longer it sits) or freeze it in an airtight container for up to 2 months (defrost in the refrigerator for up to a day before serving). Gently rewarm the stew in a heavy pot set over low heat before serving.

SERVES 6 TO 8

2 tablespoons canola oil

1 red onion, thinly sliced

3 garlic cloves, minced

2 tablespoons Xawaash Spice Mix (page 74)

2 tablespoons tomato paste

2 teaspoons kosher salt, plus more as needed

2 cups water

2 pounds boneless beef chuck or other stew meat, cut into bite-sized pieces

2 baking potatoes, cut into bite-sized pieces

2 large carrots, cut into thin coins

1 red bell pepper, stemmed, seeded, and cut into thin strips

Cooked rice, hot sauce (such as Somali Cilantro and Green Chile Pepper Sauce, page 80), cilantro leaves, lime wedges, and fresh bananas, for serving

Warm the oil in a large Dutch oven or other heavy pot set over medium heat. Add the onion and garlic and cook, stirring occasionally, until just beginning to soften, about 3 minutes. Stir in the Xawaash, tomato paste, and salt and cook until aromatic, about 1 minute. Stir in the water and increase the heat to high. Bring to a boil, reduce the heat to low, then stir in the beef and potatoes. Partially cover the pot (leave the lid slightly ajar so steam can escape) and simmer until the beef and potatoes are just cooked through, about 45 minutes. Stir in the carrots and bell pepper and cook, covered, until the beef and vegetables are all very tender, an additional 30 minutes. Season the stew to taste with salt and serve over rice with hot sauce and cilantro for topping, lime wedges for squeezing over, and bananas for eating alongside. Leftovers can be stored in an airtight container in the refrigerator for up to a few days and rewarmed in a heavy pot set over low heat (stir while you heat).

Shaah Cadays

(SOMALI SPICED TEA WITH MILK)

Essentially Somali chai, this spiced tea with milk is served most often during the Somali after-noon tea tradition known as casariya. The most important things to serve with shaah cadays are sheeko, which is the Somali term for stories. Just like Ma Gehennet's Buna (Eritrean Coffee, page 54), shaah is as much about whom you're sharing it with as it is about what's in your teacup. It's all about community and conversation. Shaah cadays is also enjoyed in the morning for breakfast with Canjeero (Sourdough Pancakes, page 83).

SERVES 4

One 1-inch piece ginger

Two 2-inch pieces cinnamon stick

5 green cardamom pods

5 whole cloves

1 teaspoon black peppercorns

2 cups cold water

3 tablespoons loose black tea
(or 4 black tea bags)

3 tablespoons granulated sugar,
plus more as needed

2 cups whole milk

Crush the ginger with the bottom of a heavy pot or the blunt edge of a knife and set aside. Place the cinnamon, cardamom, cloves, and peppercorns in a mortar and crush with a pestle until coarsely ground (or crush on a countertop or on a cutting board with the bottom of a heavy pot). Transfer the spices to a medium saucepan set over medium heat and cook, stirring, until very fragrant, about 1 minute. Add the ginger, water, tea, and sugar and increase the heat to high. Once bubbles form around the edge, immediately reduce the heat to low and let the mixture simmer for 5 minutes. Stir in the milk and let it cook for just 1 minute to warm the milk, then turn off the heat. Strain through a fine-mesh sieve into a teapot, pitcher, or straight into tea mugs. Serve immedi-ately while hot and add more sugar to taste if you'd like.

Chapter Three

Kenya

Kenya, home to about fifty million people, is a varied country defined by multiple cultures and communities. While it's well known for its Maasai culture, the Maasai actually make up only a small part of Kenya's population. Larger swaths of the population include the Swahili on the coast, Nilotic communities in the northwest, and Bantu communities in the western and central parts of the country. Mombasa, Kenya's oldest city, sits on the coast and was the country's first capital. Nairobi, its largest city and center of commerce, is now the capital (Nairobi is also home to Kibera, one of the world's largest slums). Kisumu City is the country's third largest city, followed by Eldoret and Nakuru.

The first people known to call what we now know as Kenya home were Nilotic-speaking pastoralists who migrated from present-day Sudan around 500 BCE. Kenya was a British colony for nearly a century, starting in 1888 with the arrival of the Imperial British East Africa Company and concluding with the establishment of Kenya's independence in 1963. During this period, the British brought many Indians across the Indian Ocean to work on railroads; these laborers brought their culinary culture with them, and much of this can still be seen—and tasted—throughout the country today.

The colonial period was marked by dispute and a nationalist movement that was foreshadowed by the Mau Mau revolution, which started in 1952 (the Mau Mau were also known as the Kenya Land and Freedom Army). After declaring independence from Britain, Kenya remained a member of the British-led Commonwealth of Nations, a political association whose members are almost all former UK territories. Kenya's current constitution was put into place in 2010 (the first time it had been revamped since the approval of the 1963 independence constitution).

Jomo Kenyatta became Kenya's first president following independence in 1963; he served until his death in 1978. There was a lot of corruption during his tenure. After his death, Daniel arap Moi took over the presidency and served until 2002. Uhuru Kenyatta, the son of Jomo Kenyatta, is the country's fourth and current president. Each of Kenya's nearly fifty semi-autonomous counties is governed by an elected governor.

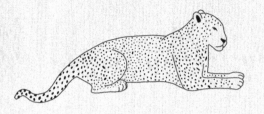

Geography and Climate

Kenya sits snugly on the East African coastline south of Ethiopia, east of Uganda, north of Tanzania, and west (and sort-of southwest) of Somalia. Outside its coastline, the country mostly consists of low plains and central highlands. The Great Rift Valley bisects the Kenyan highlands, which includes an arable plateau to the east of the valley that is home to Kenya's agricultural region, one of the most fertile in the entire continent. Mount Kenya, the second-highest peak on the continent, after Mount Kilimanjaro in Tanzania, is also located in the Kenyan Highlands. Since Kenya straddles the equator, its climate varies. The coast is hot and humid, while the inland areas are hot but much drier and the mountainous areas more temperate.

Economy and Resources

Kenya's economy is the second largest in the region (just behind Ethiopia's). Nairobi, its capital city, is the center of commerce. Kenya's coastline has been home to trade and exploration and includes many coastal cities, including Mombasa and Malindi.

The service industry (especially tourism) and agriculture are the Kenyan economy's largest sectors. When it comes to agriculture, tea, coffee, and fresh flowers are Kenya's biggest assets. Kenya is the third-largest exporter of cut flowers in the entire world and has over a hundred flower farms. About half its flower farms are located near Lake Naivasha, and the airport in Nairobi has a terminal dedicated solely to exporting flowers and vegetables.

The economy has shaped Kenya's population in many ways. When the British were in charge, they brought a large number of Indian workers into the country to construct a railway system. Many descendants of these workers stayed in Kenya and built Kenya's Indian communities. During the early 1900s, European farmers settled in the Kenyan highlands, which was already home to over a million Kikuyu people. The settlers banned the Kikuyu from growing coffee, one of the region's most important crops, and imposed various taxes, all of which drove out the people who were already there and forced them to flee to the cities.

Wildlife is a major resource in Kenya and a big part of what drives tourism in the country. Leopards, elephants, lions, buffalo, and rhinoceroses can be found in Kenya's national parks and game reserves, and in the Masai Mara habitat, which is also home to over a million wildebeests and hundreds of thousands of zebras that migrate across the Mara River every year. The migration is considered the seventh natural wonder of the world. Safaris are the main tourist attraction in the country; other attractions include Mount Kenya, tea and coffee plantations, beaches along the Swahili coast, and historical mosques.

People

Thanks to rapid population growth, nearly three-quarters of the approximately fifty million people who call Kenya home are under the age of thirty. Its population is one of the most diverse in Africa and includes about 47 distinct communities. The largest groups are the Bantus and Nilotes. The largest ethnic groups are the Kikuyu, Luhya, Kalenjin, Luo, Kamba, Kisii, Mijikenda, Meru, Turkana, and Maasai. The country also has many residents from Somalia, Asia, and Europe, making it a hub for the region's development sector.

Language

There are nearly seventy languages spoken within the country. English and Swahili are the two official languages, but many Kenyans also speak native languages such as Kiswahili and Kikuyu.

Religion

Most Kenyans are Christian (about half of whom are Protestant), and the country has the largest number of Quakers in the world. Islam is the second-largest religion; the majority of Kenyan Muslims live on the coast. Kenya also has large Hindu and Baha'i populations and a small Buddhist community.

Ma Penny

HOME
Lowell, Massachusetts

HER RECIPES
Mukimo (Mashed Green Split Peas, Corn, and Potatoes, page 118)

Sautéed Cabbage (page 117)

Why did you choose to make mukimo to share with us?

It's easy and it's one of the most common meals we make, so it's something that reminds me more of where we have been. It's something, even every time I go home [to Kenya], it's one of the first things I have to eat, mukimo. My kids love it. That's why I chose to make it instead of anything else.

What food or dish do you think best represents Kenyan food?

It depends on what tribe you're from. If we're talking about the Kikuyu, I would say it's mukimo. When you're talking about the Luhya people, which is a different tribe, they would of course say ugali [a traditional stiff cornmeal porridge]. And they do fish a lot. So, every tribe has its own things they like. Every tribe has its own liking. We are all different. One thing about the Kikuyu people is that their food isn't spicy. They have no spices. Even though people are now starting to buy them, but traditionally it's no spices. It's the cheapest of the cheapest food. It's just stuff you get from your backyard.

What's most misunderstood about the country?

I think it's security, I think. Yeah. And the poverty is there. The gap between the poor and the rich—that's not misunderstood. So, when people say, "Oh, we're not as poor as they show . . ." when they go to take the pictures. Of course, we know the gap between the rich and poor is there. The corruption is real. I don't think it's a misconception. The rich get richer. Everything I've heard about Kenya is real. I don't try to defend it because I've lived it.

How often do you cook and do you enjoy cooking?

I do cook quite a bit. I have a very busy schedule. My Mondays through Fridays get to be very wild, but I do cook. I'd say I cook every other day. It's not three meals a day. Breakfast is never here because no one is here. I only have one [child] at home now; she's out by 7:30 in the morning. So is my husband. So, usually, breakfast we don't do. Lunch I'm at work. Myself, I don't have time to eat lunch. So, we only do dinner. So, I cook every other night. But my husband cooks more. He cooks even when there's no one here to eat!

What do your children cook?

They make macaroni and cheese. My son makes Alfredo. Chicken Alfredo. But he just learned that after he went to college with a bunch of boys. But usually they don't cook too much. Their mother cooks for them!

What does passing on food traditions to your kids mean to you?

It helps me get the culture alive to my kids. And even when we visit [Kenya], they don't feel so lost.

What does home cooking mean to you?

It's healthier. When I buy food out now, the cholesterol is huge. When I cook at home, I know it's more original. And cooking is fun; it's relaxing. On Friday nights, we usually go out.

Is that date night?

No. We take everybody! Whoever is home goes.

That's a good reason to come home on Fridays.

Yes, yes. And it's good for me because I don't have time to cook

on Fridays.

How do you define community?

It gets us together. It reminds us of where we're from. When we first came in the '90s, we had more parties, but we were younger. Now we only have parties for weddings or if there's something going on.

Getting together and actually supporting each other. In my society, in the Kenyan world, let's say you had somebody here who has died or has an emergency. You can never say somebody won't be able to go home [to Kenya]. We always come together. It doesn't matter where you go to church or where you worship, it doesn't matter. We always get together. We always get the funds together. That's more what's going on in our community now. People are always ready to help.

So, help and support?

Yes, support financially or if you have an ailment or if you need someone to take you to an appointment. What happens here with people—it's like, do they know you and do you show up? It's a community thing. Do I show up for other people? If you never show up, don't expect others [to show up for you]. You're judged only by how much you give.

And by sending home, you mean flying someone back to Kenya?

Yes. And for some people who die here [in the United States], they might not have anyone here. We are it. So, if a body is here and the family is at home [in Kenya] and needs to bury them, one of us will go and bring them. We will get the funds. We've been able to do things like that in unfortunate situations.

Looking back, what are you most proud of?

Wow. In my culture? In America?

In your life.

The opportunity to come here. You appreciate more what you have at home. If I had stayed home, I would have thought everything is just given. I was raised that way until I came here and had to go to work and look for money myself. I grew up a lot, and I appreciate that very much. If I had stayed at home, I don't think I would be where I am today. Everything would be just given to me.

Ma Wambui

HOME
Nairobi, Kenya

HER RECIPE
Mukimo with Onions and Greens (page 124)

Why did you choose to make mukimo?

Mukimo is a traditional dish, and actually we eat it every day [*smiles*]. That is why I chose it. Mukimo is basically made of four main ingredients: maize [corn], beans, potatoes, and some greens. It's quite simple because all you have to do is mix them, boil, and mash. But you have to be careful not to overcook anything.

What is most misunderstood about Kenya?

That our food is bland and uninteresting. It's not! It's very, very good, and it's very wholesome, which is more important than the looks. It's good. We don't eat fast food. We eat wholesome food.

How often do you cook, and do you enjoy cooking?

I cook over the weekends. I've always cooked, and now that I'm sort of retired, I don't want to forget my cooking.

Do your children and grandchildren cook?

My children do cook—I taught them. Some of my grandchildren are interested. My hope is for my children to teach their children.

What does passing on food traditions mean to you?

It means a lot. It's very important. We believe our food is good and it must continue because it's wholesome and healthy and everything that's going on today with children and their health. It's important to me that our children eat our traditional food.

What does home mean to you?

Where the family lives. It's where you live, and it's where your destiny is in life.

How do you define community?

A collection of people living together. Africans have always lived in communities, in villages. We have people, neighbors, around us. There's the family community and an extended community, where a whole village lives and supports each other.

Looking back, what are you most proud of?

I am proud of being Kenyan. It's a beautiful country with a lot of resources and good weather, and our traditions are good, and our children are taught to obey and respect their parents and to participate in home activities. It's a great country all around, and I'm proud to be a Kenyan.

What was your favorite meal growing up?

Rice! Because we didn't have it often, so I looked forward to rice, especially with stew. I also used to love chapattis [flatbreads], which we only ate when there was something happening at home or in the village.

And who used to cook those?

My mother.

Is she the one who taught you to cook?

Yes.

What do you think of the gender roles in Kenya? What does it mean to be a woman in Kenya?

The role of a woman is key to the family. The woman takes care of the family, brings up the children, cooks. The man is out. So, it is the woman who brings up the family and keeps the family together. She is the mecca for family, for society.

Ma Kauthar

HOME
Lamu Island, Kenya

HER RECIPES
Mango Chile Sauce (page 116)
Chicken Biryani (page 122)
Basboosa (Semolina Cake, page 128)
Fresh Carrot Drink (page 129)

Which dish do you think best represents Kenyan food?

The one thing I would say identifies Swahili food is pilau [a rice-based dish]. Pilau can be different, like meat pilau, chicken pilau, and even vegetable pilau. The traditional way is using meat. The key to great pilau is to make your spice mix from scratch. These days, everyone uses store-bought spices or uses the blender to make things faster. If you take your time and pound things individually like I do, sauté the ingredients and spices one at a time instead of throwing it all together, it will turn out to be the best pilau. It's like Indians and biryani. Pilau is what identifies us Swahili people in Kenya. We also eat coconut rice a lot and vegetables with roasted meat or grilled black pepper chicken. The pilipili ya ku kukaanga (roasted chile sauce) accompanies almost all our dishes.

Cuisine in Lamu is heavy on coconut. Someone can use three coconuts to just one small vegetable dish. The use is classic and of high quality. Our seafood is fresh. It is straight from the ocean to our table, and that is what makes our food really good. I can go elsewhere and cook the same dish with the same ingredients, but it doesn't taste the same.

How often do you cook, and do you enjoy cooking?

I have been here for thirteen years, but I have only started cooking for money recently. It's a hobby. It's something I love. My nephew Hakim noticed that I loved cooking, but I didn't have the opportunity to sell my food. If someone wanted a dish cooked, I would volunteer and just do it for them. Hakim approached me and said, "How about I open a community restaurant, and you can cook in it?" I agreed, not thinking it would go anywhere. Hakim started the Maskani Youth Initiative, a local program led by the youth of Shela village and Lamu as a way to give young people a space to call their own. A café occupies part of that space, and that is where people can go to eat my food. Sometimes we get big orders and other times small orders. We are slowly beginning to get known in the community. So, I cook here and send it to the restaurant or wherever people want.

Looking back, what are you most proud of?

I am proud to be a housewife. I have my house, I take care of my children, and I make people happy with my food. So that is what I am most proud of.

What would you say distinguishes the women of Lamu?

I am originally from Mombasa (another coastal city), but I have been living in Lamu for thirteen years. The women in Lamu are different in the way they dress and talk. Even if they move from Lamu to the UK for years, you can just tell. The culture is different because people are more modest; it is a very conservative society. They keep their traditions. Women cover up and have high respect for themselves. Most of the people here are like family. Everyone knows each other here because it's a small place. For example, in Mombasa, you can go out and dress however you want, and no one really cares. Here, your reputation and that of your family is everything. So, you can't go out looking however.

Kachumbari

(TOMATO AND ONION SALAD)

This crunchy, fresh salad is popular in Kenya but is also eaten throughout East Africa. You'll find similar versions in Tanzania and beyond. Its main components are tomatoes and onions, but cucumbers and avocado are regular additions, so we went with them here, since we are the-more-the-merrier types. You can also add some minced fresh chiles if you'd like. Serve with just about anything you can think of, from fish like Roti ya Houma Pampa (Salt Cod with Tomatoes and Onions, page 264) to chicken like Doro Wat (Stewed Chicken Legs with Berbere and Eggs, page 53) or alongside legumes or beans like Kunde (Black-Eyed Peas and Tomatoes in Peanut Sauce, page 127) with some rice for a vegan meal. If you wait to add the avocado until you serve, you can make the salad up to a few hours in advance and just keep it covered at room temperature. Stir in the avocado just before serving.

SERVES 4

1 tablespoon kosher salt, plus more as needed

1 cup boiling water

1 small red onion, thinly sliced into half-moons

2 large tomatoes, diced

1 cucumber, peeled, seeded and diced

3 tablespoons freshly squeezed lime juice

1 ripe avocado, pitted, peeled, and diced

Dissolve the salt in the boiling water in a small bowl. Add the onion and mix well. Let the onion soak while you chop the rest of your vegetables. This soaking will reduce the intensity of the raw onion.

Once the onion has soaked for at least 10 minutes, drain and transfer it to a medium bowl. Add the tomatoes, cucumber, and lime juice and stir well to combine. Season the vegetables to taste with salt if needed (it will depend on how much salt the onions held on to). Gently stir in the avocado and serve immediately.

Mango Chile Sauce

Ma Kauthar told us that this chile sauce is served with every main dish, from her Chicken Biryani (page 122) to stews, curries, and more. It's also delicious on eggs. Like all hot sauces, this one can be adjusted by adding more chiles to make it spicier or using fewer to make it milder. We find that two jalapeños give it zip without being too overwhelming. Also note that this sauce thickens considerably as it cools (mango has a good amount of natural pectin in it), so no worries if it seems a little loose while it's still hot.

MAKES ABOUT 1½ CUPS

1 unripe mango (it should be incredibly firm to the touch), pitted, peeled, and coarsely chopped

4 medium vine-ripened tomatoes, coarsely chopped

2 jalapeños, stemmed and coarsely chopped (use less or leave out if you don't want things too spicy)

2 tablespoons tomato paste

2 tablespoons freshly squeezed lemon juice, plus more as needed

2 tablespoons canola oil

1 teaspoon kosher salt, plus more as needed

½ cup water

In the jar of a blender, combine the mango, tomatoes, jalapeños, tomato paste, lemon juice, oil, salt, and water and puree until smooth. Transfer the mixture to a small saucepan and set it uncovered over high heat. Bring the sauce to a boil, reduce the heat to low, and simmer, stirring occasionally to keep the sauce from burning, until the sauce is thick enough to coat a spoon, about 20 minutes. Let the sauce cool to room temperature, then season to taste with additional salt and/or lemon juice if needed. Serve immediately or store in an airtight container in the refrigerator for up to a week.

MA PENNY'S

Sautéed Cabbage

When Ma Penny prepared her signature dish, Mukimo (Mashed Green Split Peas, Corn, and Potatoes, page 118), she also quickly sautéed this green cabbage to serve with it. She says she always serves mukimo with green cabbage because the mukimo can dry out quickly as it cools down and the cabbage retains moisture and keeps the meal more balanced. It's also a wonderfully quick, healthy, and easy side dish. Her husband, the main cook in the kitchen, walked in as she was cooking it, and she told us that he makes it better than she does. He said he adds sweet white onions to his cabbage and then added, "We try many ways." The best home kitchens are indeed the flexible ones.

SERVES 6

3 tablespoons extra-virgin olive oil

1 green cabbage, thinly sliced

2 teaspoons seasoned salt (such as Lawry's), or 1 teaspoon kosher salt plus 1 teaspoon sweet paprika

Warm the oil in a large skillet set over medium heat. Add the cabbage, sprinkle with the seasoned salt, and cook, stirring occasionally, until just softened and a tiny bit brown in spots, about 10 minutes. Serve immediately, while hot. Leftovers can be stored in an airtight container in the refrigerator and rewarmed in a skillet set over low heat.

Mukimo

(MASHED GREEN SPLIT PEAS, CORN, AND POTATOES)

As Ma Penny explained, she chose to share this traditional dish of mashed split peas, potatoes, and corn with us because it's convenient, healthy, fast, and her most favorite food. It's also a lesson in using what's available in America to mimic the flavors left behind in Kenya. As she said, "It's not a food we abandoned when we came here. In Kenya, we'd go to the garden and pick the peas and peel them, but here in America we use what we have, which is Goya dried split peas." Then she continued, "And potatoes are just potatoes everywhere." Mukimo is an affordable dish, but she says it's even more so in Kenya, because you "just go to your backyard." Ma Penny is also unabashed about her love for her handheld electric mixer. "In Kenya, we'd use a pot made of clay and a stick to mix up the mukimo. Here I use an electric mixer! We have different things, but it's the same meal no matter what." Be sure to cook the peas and potatoes in separate pots, since they have different cooking times. This is best served with Ma Penny's Sautéed Cabbage (page 117) and any type of stewed or roasted meat, such as Ma Halima's Beef Suqaar (page 84).

SERVES 6

One 16-ounce package dried green split peas, rinsed well and drained

1 pound red potatoes, coarsely chopped and rinsed well

Half a 500-gram/8-ounce bag frozen jumbo corn kernels (often labeled Choclo Desgranado), or one 15-ounce can hominy, drained and rinsed well

2 tablespoons unsalted butter

2 teaspoons kosher salt, plus more as needed

Place the split peas in a large pot, cover with water, set over high heat, and bring to a boil. Reduce the heat to low and simmer until the peas are soft and tender and have burst, 45 minutes to 1 hour. Carefully drain them in a fine-mesh sieve. (Ma Penny says that in Africa, people have "kitchen hands," so they don't have to use oven mitts or towels—but, she says, you should.) Make sure the peas are very well drained (you don't want the mukimo to be watery). Set the peas aside.

Meanwhile, place the potatoes in a separate large pot, cover with water, set over high heat, and bring to a boil. Reduce the heat to low and simmer until the potatoes are tender, about 20 minutes. Drain the potatoes in a colander, shaking the colander a few times to make sure you've gotten rid of all the excess water. Set the potatoes aside.

Fill a medium pot (the last pot, promise!) with water, bring to a boil, and add the corn. Cook just until the kernels are warmed through, about 5 minutes. Drain the corn and set aside.

Place the well-drained peas and potatoes in one of the empty pots and use a handheld mixer ("every kitchen should have one of these," says Ma Penny) or a potato masher to thoroughly blend the peas and potatoes together until they're completely combined and quite smooth, almost like green mashed potatoes. Whip in the butter and salt and then season to taste with more salt if needed. Stir in the corn. Serve immediately, while hot. Leftovers can be stored in the refrigerator for up to a week and rewarmed in the microwave or in a heavy pot set over low heat (stir while you heat).

Sukuma Wiki

(GREENS WITH TOMATOES)

These well-seasoned greens are similar to collards, which, with their fragrant potlikker, are popular in the American South and are a reminder of the undeniably deep threads that tie together African and African American cooking. *Sukuma wiki* means "to stretch the week"—in other words, using these greens, which are affordable and readily available, can help stretch any meal a bit further. Greens are a staple in Kenyan cooking and in most East African cooking in general. Serve this dish with rice for a traditional, healthy, and completely vegan meal.

SERVES 4

2 tablespoons canola oil

1 large yellow onion, finely diced

1 teaspoon ground cumin

½ teaspoon ground coriander

½ teaspoon ground turmeric

2 large tomatoes, coarsely chopped

1 pound kale and/or collards (or any dark leafy greens), tough stems discarded, leaves coarsely chopped

Kosher salt

½ cup water

2 tablespoons freshly squeezed lemon juice

Warm the oil in a large Dutch oven or other heavy pot set over medium heat. Add the onion, cumin, coriander, and turmeric and cook, stirring, until the onion begins to soften, about 5 minutes. Add the tomatoes, greens, a large pinch of salt, and the water. Stir everything well to combine, cover, and simmer until the greens are very tender and soft, about 15 minutes. Turn off the heat, stir in the lemon juice, season the greens to taste with salt, and serve immediately. Leftovers can be stored in an airtight container in the refrigerator for up to a few days and rewarmed in a heavy pot set over low heat (stir while you heat).

Chicken Biryani

Making biryani is a labor of love, and the layering of flavor pays off. When Ma Kauthar showed us how she prepares this, she did the whole thing outdoors and included an option that infused the dish with a big dose of smoky flavor. She put a small metal container with oil directly in the pot, nestled right into the layers of rice and chicken, and then placed a hot coal directly in the container with the oil. She covered the pot, and the smoke from that little container wove its way into the whole dish. She then placed more hot coals on top of the lid of the pot, as in true Dutch oven cooking. "This is real barbecue!" she told us. In an effort to make the biryani easier to make indoors, we opted to just put the covered pot in the oven.

SERVES 4 TO 6

3 medium vine-ripened tomatoes

Canola oil, for frying

2 large red onions, thinly sliced into half-moons

1 pound Yukon gold potatoes, quartered

4 green bell peppers, stemmed, seeded, and coarsely chopped

1 cup long-grain white rice (preferably basmati)

4 cups water

2 star anise pods (optional)

One 2-inch piece cinnamon stick

3 green cardamom pods

1 tablespoon plus 1 teaspoon kosher salt

3 garlic cloves, minced

One 2-inch piece ginger, peeled and minced

1 tablespoon tomato paste

3 large carrots, coarsely grated

Preheat the oven to 350°F.

Cut off and discard a thin slice from the stem end of each tomato and then coarsely grate the tomatoes on a box grater directly into a bowl. Discard the skins.

Heat 2 inches of oil in a Dutch oven or other heavy pot set over medium-high heat until it reaches 375°F on an instant-read thermometer or until a piece of onion sizzles on contact. Add the onion and cook, stirring occasionally, until golden brown and crisp, about 15 minutes. Use a slotted spoon to transfer the onion to a colander set over a bowl to drain.

Carefully add the potatoes to the hot oil and cook, stirring occasionally, until the potatoes are crisp on the outside, about 8 minutes (they won't be completely cooked through). Transfer the potatoes to the colander with the onion and let them drain.

Add the bell peppers to the hot oil and cook, stirring occasionally, until the peppers are tender and go from bright green to more of a khaki, about 3 minutes. Transfer the peppers to the colander with the potatoes and onion and let them drain.

Reserve 5 tablespoons of the cooking oil and allow the rest to cool before storing it for another use or discarding it.

2 tablespoons Xawaash Spice Mix (page 74)

1 chicken or vegetable bouillon cube

2 pounds boneless, skinless chicken thighs and/or breasts, cut into bite-sized pieces

Large handful of cilantro leaves, coarsely chopped

Place the rice in a fine-mesh sieve and rinse with cold tap water, stirring the rice gently with your hands, until the water runs clear, about 1 minute.

Fill a medium pot with water. Bring the water to a boil and add the star anise (if using), the cinnamon, cardamom, and 1 tablespoon of the salt. Add the rice to the pot and cook, uncovered, until it is barely tender, about 10 minutes.

Drain the cooked rice in a colander or fine-mesh sieve (if using a colander, make sure the holes aren't too big), rinse with cool water to stop the cooking, then set it aside.

Place 4 tablespoons of the reserved cooking oil in a large heavy pot set over high heat. Add the garlic and ginger and cook, stirring, until they're sizzling and fragrant, about 30 seconds. Add the tomato paste and stir, until it's incorporated with the oil, about 30 seconds. Add the grated tomatoes and cook, stirring, until most of the moisture from the tomatoes has evaporated, about 2 minutes. Add half the grated carrot and the spice mix, then use your fingers to crumble in the bouillon cube. Stir well to combine and then stir in the chicken and remaining 1 teaspoon salt. Cover the pot and cook until the chicken is just opaque on the outside and about halfway cooked through, about 10 minutes.

Spread the remaining 1 tablespoon oil over the surface of a large oven-safe pot and add half the rice (remove and discard any whole spices you see). Stir together the peppers, potatoes, and onion in the colander and place half the mixture over the rice. Evenly sprinkle half the remaining carrot and half the cilantro on top. Place half the chicken with its cooking juices on top of everything. Repeat the layering process one more time. Cover the pot and place in the oven. Bake until the chicken, rice, and potatoes are completely cooked through and incredibly fragrant, about 30 minutes. Remove the biryani from the oven and let it sit, covered, for 10 minutes before uncovering. Mix everything together and serve immediately. Leftovers can be stored in an airtight container in the refrigerator for up to a few days and rewarmed in a heavy pot set over low heat (stir while you heat).

Mukimo with Onions and Greens

Two recipes for mukimo in one book might seem like overkill, but we found it fascinating to see the difference between Ma Penny's version, made at home in Massachusetts, and Ma Wambui's, made at home in Kenya. Whereas Ma Penny uses green split peas, potatoes, and corn, Ma Wambui uses beans instead of split peas and makes her mukimo green with a vibrant puree of cooked greens, adding sweet sautéed onions for another layer of flavor. We like both versions equally, and including them both in this book serves as a reminder that there's no one right way to make anything and that multiple perspectives and choices are what make cooking so endlessly interesting. "This dish on its own is wholesome and can be served by itself as a meal, if need be," Ma Wambui says, "or serve in scoops with beef or chicken stew."

SERVES 6

2 tablespoons canola oil

1 red onion, finely chopped

Kosher salt

1 pound dark leafy greens (like kale or collards), tough stems discarded, leaves finely chopped

1½ pounds Yukon gold potatoes, coarsely chopped

One 15-ounce can butter, broad, fava, or cannellini beans, drained and rinsed

Half a 500-gram/8-ounce bag frozen jumbo corn kernels (often labeled Choclo Desgranado), or one 15-ounce can hominy, drained and rinsed well

Warm the oil in a large skillet set over medium heat. Add the onion and cook, stirring occasionally, until soft and translucent, about 10 minutes. Season the onion with a large sprinkle of salt, turn off the heat, and set the skillet aside.

Bring a large pot of water to a boil and add the greens. Cook, stirring occasionally, until very tender, about 15 minutes. Use a handheld strainer to remove the greens from the pot and transfer them, along with ½ cup of the cooking liquid, to the jar of a blender or to a food processor. Leave the rest of the cooking water in the pot. Add 1 teaspoon of the salt to the blender or food processor and puree until smooth (take caution when pureeing the hot mixture). Set the mixture aside.

Place the potatoes in the pot of hot water you used to cook the greens and add 1 tablespoon salt. Bring the water to a boil, reduce the heat to low, and simmer until the potatoes are just beginning to get tender, about 8 minutes. Add the beans and cook until both the potatoes and beans are soft enough to mash, about 10 minutes. During the last minute of cooking, add the corn, just to warm the kernels. Use a teacup or measuring pitcher to collect about 1 cup of the cooking liquid and reserve it. Drain the potatoes, beans, and corn and return them to the empty pot. Use a potato masher

to crush the mixture together until it's very smooth. Add the cooked onion and pureed greens to the potato mixture. If the mixture is too thick for your liking, thin it out with some of the reserved potato cooking liquid (depending on how thick you like it, you might not use the entire cup). Stir very well to combine and season the mukimo to taste with salt. Transfer the mukimo to a serving dish. If you'd like, use the tines of a fork to make a decorative pattern on the surface of the mukimo. Serve immediately. Leftovers can be stored in an airtight container in the refrigerator for up to a week and warmed in the microwave or in a heavy pot set over low heat (stir while you heat).

Kunde

(BLACK-EYED PEAS AND TOMATOES IN PEANUT SAUCE)

Kunde is the Swahili word for black-eyed peas or cowpeas. Serve these stewed peas, fragrant with tomatoes and peanuts, with cooked rice for a quick, affordable, very filling, and totally vegan meal. Feel free to add some diced sweet potatoes or peeled and chopped winter squash to the pot, along with some chopped dark leafy greens (like kale or collards), if you want to stretch the beans into a heartier and even healthier dish. Just simmer until the vegetables are tender.

SERVES 4 AS A MAIN DISH, 6 AS A SIDE DISH

¼ cup unsalted roasted peanuts, or 3 tablespoons creamy peanut butter

2 tablespoons canola oil

1 yellow onion, finely chopped

1 teaspoon ground coriander

1 teaspoon ground turmeric

1 large tomato, finely chopped

Kosher salt

Two 15.5-ounce cans black-eyed peas, drained and rinsed

½ cup water

If using whole peanuts, place them in a food processor and pulse until finely ground, almost like sand. Set the peanuts aside.

Warm the oil in a medium saucepan set over medium heat. Add the onion and cook, stirring occasionally, until it begins to soften, about 5 minutes. Add the coriander and turmeric and cook, stirring, until fragrant, about 30 seconds. Add the tomato and a large pinch of salt and cook, stirring occasionally, until the liquid from the tomato has evaporated and the mixture is quite dry, about 5 minutes. Add the peas, peanuts (or peanut butter, if using), and water, increase the heat to high, and bring the mixture to a boil. Reduce the heat to low and simmer just until the peas have absorbed some of the wonderful flavor, about 5 minutes. Season the peas to taste with salt and serve immediately, while hot. Leftovers can be stored in an airtight container in the refrigerator for up to a few days and rewarmed in a heavy pot set over low heat (stir while you heat).

Basboosa

(SEMOLINA CAKE)

Basboosa (sometimes spelled 'basbousa' and sometimes called 'nammoura' throughout the Middle East) is a very sweet and moist cake made with semolina flour, with the addition of a sugar syrup that can be flavored with anything from orange flower water to cardamom or rose water. This cake is popular in Middle Eastern countries, in Arab, Turkish, and Greek kitchens, and also in East African countries that have a Middle Eastern influence (which is most of them). Ma Kauthar's version uses plenty of cardamom, coconut, vanilla, and almonds for texture and flavor. Serve with hot coffee or tea.

SERVES 12

1 cup water

1¾ cups granulated sugar

1 teaspoon ground cardamom

1 teaspoon freshly squeezed lime juice

4 large eggs

1 teaspoon baking powder

½ cup canola oil

1 cup all-purpose flour

1 cup buttermilk (or ¾ cup plain yogurt and ¼ cup water whisked together)

½ teaspoon pure vanilla extract (preferably from Madagascar or Comoros)

1 cup semolina flour

1 cup unsweetened coconut flakes

½ cup blanched slivered almonds

Preheat the oven to 350°F. Spray a 9 by 13-inch baking dish with nonstick spray and line the dish with parchment paper.

Place the water, ¾ cup of the sugar, and ½ teaspoon of the cardamom in a small pot set over high heat. Bring to a boil and stir until the sugar is dissolved, about 1 minute, then boil the syrup until slightly thickened and reduced to about ¾ cup, about 5 minutes. Turn off the heat, stir in the lime juice, and set the syrup aside.

Place the eggs in a large bowl and whisk together. Add the remaining 1 cup sugar and the baking powder and, using a handheld mixer (or a whisk and a lot of elbow grease), blend them together on high speed until the sugar is dissolved, about 3 minutes. Add the oil and all-purpose flour and beat until smooth and thick, about 1 minute. Beat in the buttermilk, vanilla, and remaining ½ teaspoon cardamom. Stir in the semolina flour and coconut flakes.

Transfer the batter to the prepared baking dish and, using a spoon, spread it into an even layer. Evenly sprinkle the almonds on top of the batter. Bake the basboosa until it is firm to the touch, a toothpick tests clean, and the top is a light golden brown, 25 to 35 minutes.

Cut the basboosa into twelve even pieces and then evenly pour the syrup over them. Let the basboosa cool and serve at room temperature. Leftovers can be stored in an airtight container at room temperature for up to a few days.

MA KAUTHAR'S

Fresh Carrot Drink

Ma Kauthar blends carrots with water and sugar, strains the mixture, and then adds lemon juice to create a refreshing drink that she refers to as her own version of Fanta soda. We love it for its color and sweet flavor. To turn it into a cocktail, add a splash of whatever spirit you most enjoy. Spiced rum would complement the carrot flavor well.

SERVES 4

4 large carrots (about 1¼ pounds), coarsely grated or finely chopped

¼ cup granulated sugar, plus more if needed

4 cups water

3 tablespoons freshly squeezed lemon juice, plus more if needed

Ice, for serving

Place the carrots, sugar, and water in the jar of a blender. Blend until smooth. Pour the mixture through a fine-mesh sieve set over a pitcher and press down to extract all the liquid from the solids. Whisk in the lemon juice. Taste the mixture and add more lemon if you prefer it more tart or more sugar if you prefer it sweeter. Fill four tall glasses with ice and divide the drink among them. Serve immediately.

Chapter Four

Tanza

nia

Tanzania is a country in a few parts: It consists of a mainland in East Africa that borders the Indian Ocean, plus the island of Zanzibar (which is actually an archipelago containing many islands, including Pemba Island) and Mafia Island. Over forty-five million people call Tanzania home.

A bit of political and economic background: Tanzania, as we now know it, began when British rule ended in 1961. Tanganyika, the mainland, merged with Zanzibar in 1964 and the union was proclaimed the United Republic of Tanzania. Zanzibar is an archipelago made up of two large islands (Pemba Island and Unguja) and lots of small islands. Zanzibar remains a semiautonomous region of the country. During the merge, Tanzania remained a one-party state with a socialist approach to economic development for about two decades. Tanzania began to incorporate new political and economic reforms in the mid-1980s that resulted in the end of one-party rule in 1994.

Geography and Climate

If you're looking at a map, Tanzania's mainland sits below Uganda, Kenya, and Lake Victoria and above Mozambique, Lake Nyasa, Malawi, and Zambia. The Indian Ocean is to its right, Rwanda to its left. While Dodoma is the official capital of the country, Dar es Salaam, its largest city, is more widely known and considered Tanzania's commercial capital. A gigantic country south of the equator, the climate in Tanzania varies, but the temperatures throughout the country are usually quite hot. The humidity is what varies the most, and the tropical and coastal areas are the most humid, while the highlands are much more temperate. There are two rainy seasons, one in the spring beginning around March and the other in the fall beginning around October (both last a few months).

Economy and Resources

The Tanzanian economy is based almost exclusively on agriculture. Among its many crops, Tanzania produces cloves, coconuts, Brazil nuts, cashew nuts, coffee, tea, and tobacco. Zanzibar is commonly referred to as the Spice Islands because so many spices grow there, including black pepper, cinnamon, cloves, and nutmeg. Because its economy is based on natural resources and farming, it's also highly vulnerable to variables like unpredictable weather (which can cause the economy to surge up and down) and global warming.

Ma Shara walking to her daughter's home in Zanzibar

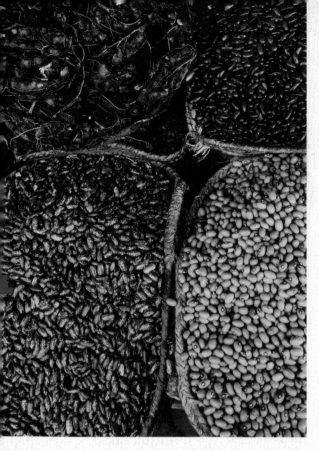

This vulnerability has meant that even though the economy has seen growth, the country remains one of the poorest in the world. In addition to economic challenges, religious tension between Christians and Muslims has fueled intermittent violence in the country.

People

Over 120 different and distinct indigenous groups make up the Tanzanian population. As the country has become progressively more modern and urban, some of the smaller groups are losing their foothold because older practices and traditions are being left behind for city living and modernization.

The San, or Saan, people were indigenous hunter-gatherers, and there's evidence of San-type hunting bands in Tanzania as early as 5000 BCE. These bands are thought to be the precursor to the Sandawe hunters of northern mainland Tanzania that preceded the Cushitic peoples from Ethiopia, who migrated there around 1000 BCE. The Cushitic peoples brought their agriculture and pastoral practices with them (the Iraqw, Mbugu, Gorowa, and Burungi all have Cushitic roots). Bantu agriculturalists arrived from the west and the south in roughly 500 CE, bringing with them their knowledge of iron. Nilotic pastoralists from the Nile Delta arrived at about the same time.

To fast-forward very quickly, the majority of Tanzanians living today descend from the Bantu. The largest group is the Sukuma, who live in the northern part of the mainland just south of Lake Victoria. Other Bantu-descended groups include the Hehe in the southern highlands, the Haya in the northwest corner, the Nyamwezi is the west-central part of the mainland, the Chaga in the mountains of the south, and the Makonde in the southeast.

There are also groups who descend from the Nilotic such as the Maasai, Arusha, Samburu, and Baraguyu. They all live in the north-central part of the mainland. The Zaramo are the most urbanized indigenous group and mostly live in Dar es Salaam and along the coastline just next to it. The smallest ethnic group, the Zanaki, live near Musoma in the Lake Victoria region. Julius Nyerere, the country's founding father and first president, who governed until 1985, was a Zanaki.

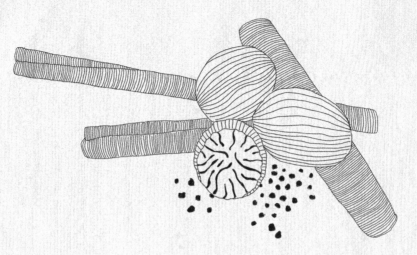

Language

Swahili (Kiswahili) and English are the country's two official languages. Swahili is actually made up of several Bantu dialects mixed with Arabic. Virtually all Tanzanians speak Swahili, and the language was heavily promoted and encouraged after independence from the British. It's the language used in the primary years of education in addition to being used in most Tanzanian literature, poetry, and theater. English is taught to older students during the higher levels of education, and it's also used in government offices.

Religion

About a third of Tanzanians are Muslim, and the majority of Muslim Tanzanians are Sunni (there is a smaller Shiite population that includes an Ismaili community). Another third of Tanzanians are Christian, which includes Baptists, Lutherans, Methodists, and Roman Catholics. The final third of the population is a bit harder to define, since they hold traditional beliefs that adhere to their indigenous religious practices.

Ma Vicky

HOME
Mount Vernon, New York

HER RECIPES
Matoke with Steamed Spinach
(Stewed Plantains with Pink Beans, Beef,
and Coconut Milk, page 150)

Ma Vicky's Famous Lasagna (page 156)

Why did you choose to make matoke?

Matoke is my staple food. I come from Bukoba in Tanzania, and around
there, it's the staple food.

When do you usually make matoke?

Whenever I'm happy, I make matoke.

What dish best represents Tanzania?

I think for the rest of the country, the main food is ugali [a traditional
stiff cornmeal porridge] and rice.

What is most misunderstood about Tanzania?

Most people think like, once people are poor, they are desperate, and they
are not happy. But like most African countries, poor people [in Tanzania]
are happy because the first thing which makes you happy is family, and
once they are around family, they can cook and eat together and they are
happy and forget their troubles. We're not as miserable as people think.

How often do you cook, and do you enjoy cooking?

I cook every day. I enjoy cooking, but growing up, I didn't cook a lot
because I was born "a princess," so I didn't have to cook. But once I
came to America, I started cooking, and now I enjoy it.

Do your children and grandchildren cook?
Yes.

Did you teach them to cook?
My mother taught them.

What does passing on food traditions mean to you?
It means a lot because that's what keeps families together. If you know how to make a dish, you can tell stories through food like, "My grandma used to make it like this," like I can tell about my grandma, and I'm a grandma now, so traditions can go on.

What does home mean to you?
Home means everything. Not just a lot. Everything.

How do you define community?
Extended family. Uncles, cousins, neighbors.

Looking back, what are you most proud of?
I'm most proud of my mom and my aunt, because I think they led me to believe that all people are very good, because they always welcomed everybody and they didn't make judgments. They just took you as you were. So, growing up with them, I thought that's how it was supposed to be. Be nice to everyone, invite everyone to your house. I learned my lesson once I got out and went to live in the city and that wasn't the case. But looking back on that makes me feel good. I learned something that was very positive.

What was your favorite meal growing up?
Matoke!

Who made it?
My grandma and my mom. But during holidays, whether it was Christmas or whatever, the food was cooked at the mosque because they made it better. So, the whole community, whether you were Muslim or Christian or whatever, we would get together.

How has your cooking changed since you moved here?

I think it has gotten better because now I can cook other dishes. I can cook Italian dishes, I can cook Indian dishes, I can cook Caribbean dishes.

Why is it important to you to cook food from Tanzania here in the US?

It makes me feel like I'm still connected, and it's the kind of food that I enjoy. I enjoy other foods but [Tanzanian] food brings me home.

What's your process of finding ingredients here? Are there any substitutions you have come up with?

Not exactly, although the matoke is not exactly the same as we have over there, but everything else is the same. You can find anything in America.

Ma Shara

What foods are most popular in your community?

We love rice in coconut sauce, and also I think most things come with
spices and coconut—both of those are our signatures in the kitchen.
Rice with coconut sauce and vegetables in coconut sauce, like spinach
with onions and garlic in coconut sauce. Fish, also. It can be fish curry or
boiled fish with some vegetables and something sour like lime. Simple.
Also, when we have special days, we'll have Indian curry. We'll deep-fry
onions, garlic, and other stuff like potatoes, tomato paste, curry powder.
We don't eat meat so often, very rarely. Our food is influenced by Indians,
Arabs, a little bit Portuguese.

What's your favorite thing to cook?

Banana stew. We prepare bananas and make fresh coconut milk and add
spices like cumin, turmeric, and fresh garlic and ginger paste. We mix it
with banana and boil it together. Sometimes we add fish. We'll prepare
the fish separately with just salt and then add it to the banana. This food
we've borrowed from another culture. It's not from Zanzibar. It's from
Comorian people, and they brought it here [see Ma Mariama's M'tsolola
on page 266].

When you were younger, was that also your favorite dish?

No, it was rice.

Who taught you how to cook?

My mom. My mom and my auntie. At first, I lived with my mom in Zanzibar, here, and then I moved to Pemba Island to get my education and lived with my auntie, so she taught me how to cook as well.

And you have how many children?

Four. I have three daughters and one son.

Did you teach your children to cook?

Yes, I have taught them. Two of them, they're good cooks.

What does passing on food traditions mean to you?

It means a lot. Because I really appreciate my culture, and I think it is very important to sustain this culture. Culture is not static. It moves—but not very quickly. So, it means a lot to me to pass these foods and how to cook them to my children and grandchildren so they can know what we eat, because there's a lot of benefits to eating what we eat. It's nutritious, healthy food, especially compared to a lot of contemporary food. I've seen the food in other parts of the world. A lot of oil, a lot of mayonnaise. A lot of man-made stuff. Chemicals. We use a few of those things, but not very much. It's important that we all stay healthy, and to stay healthy, we need to know what to eat and how to cook.

Was that the motivation for starting your cooking classes? Why did you start them?

Not only that. I'm glad for people to eat this nutritious, delicious, authentic Zanzibar food, but at the same time, I want tourists to know what Zanzibar is. Zanzibar is large. It's not just beach and sea. If you talk about culture anywhere else, you'd also be talking about cooking, eating, what people are wearing, the whole environment. How people do their things. Cooking, for us, is a major cultural point. This has made me want tourists to know more about Zanzibar at large. To not just sit on the beach, but to come enjoy a meal and see how we cook in our homes. I don't cook in a restaurant, I cook at home. So, people can see not just what we cook, but how we live. So, tourists can see how we live. The authentic Zanzibar life. So, when they go home, they can have a memory of not just the beach and the snorkeling and the luxurious hotels, but the actual Zanzibar. Traditional Zanzibar.

What is special about the community here? What makes it different than other places?

Connection between individuals. People are united. We have a sense of community. You get up in the morning, you go outside, you stop by your neighbor and see how they are. Are they well? Are they having a problem? There's a sense of community and love of each other. Whether you're Christian or Muslim, there's love. There's little conflict, which makes it different than other places that have so much conflict. We do things together. If your neighbor is ill, you help your neighbor.

What is most misunderstood about Zanzibar?

Not all people who are in Zanzibar are Zanzibarians. And sometimes they take advantage of tourists here, and the misconception can sometimes be that Zanzibar isn't safe. You see on the internet sometimes that if you go to Zanzibar you have to be very careful, that people might steal your stuff. But our traditions here are to be kind. When one person does something bad, it can spoil the whole of Zanzibar.

Anything else you want to add?

I would say Zanzibar is a nice place to come and visit, but when you come, don't just stay in the hotels. Get outside of the hotel and do different kinds of activities. Take a tour of a village, take a cooking class, go to centers for people who have special needs and visit with them. Find out more. Ask more. Ask what different things you can do apart from just the popular things that you see on the internet from every tour operator website. There are other unique things to do outside.

Ndizi Kaanga

(FRIED PLANTAINS)

As Ma Vicky taught us, plantains are a huge part of Tanzanian cooking, and there are tons of varietals and different ways of preparing each. These simple fried plantains are best made with bright yellow plantains that are somewhere in between the firm, starchy, underripe green plantains and the super-soft, super-sweet, almost-black overripe plantains. Fried in a little butter or ghee and finished with a splash of fresh lemon juice and a sprinkle of both salt and nutmeg, these plantains ride the line between sweet and savory. Serve on their own for a snack or alongside Zanzibar Pilau (Rice Pilaf, page 148), cooked vegetables, and grilled meat or fish for a complete meal. You could even sprinkle them with a bit of brown sugar as they cook, finish them with a splash of rum, and serve with vanilla ice cream for a Tanzanian version of bananas Foster.

SERVES 4

3 tablespoons unsalted butter or ghee

2 large yellow plantains, peeled and cut into 1-inch-thick pieces on the diagonal

2 tablespoons freshly squeezed lemon juice, plus additional for squeezing over

½ teaspoon kosher salt

Pinch of freshly grated nutmeg

Place the butter in a large nonstick skillet set over medium-high heat. Once the butter has melted, add the plantain pieces and cook until dark brown on the undersides, about 2 minutes. Carefully turn each piece of plantain and cook just until the second sides are lightly browned, about another minute. Transfer the plantains, cut-sides up, to a serving platter. Drizzle with the lemon juice and sprinkle with the salt and nutmeg. Serve immediately with the extra lemon for squeezing over. Leftovers can be stored in a container in the refrigerator for up to a few days and rewarmed in a skillet before serving.

Ajemi Bread with Carrots and Green Pepper

This bread, peppered with colorful and crunchy vegetables, likely became popular in Tanzania because of Arabic settlers from Yemen. Like other flatbreads in the book, such as Sabaayad (Somali Flatbreads, page 76), these are simple and satisfying to make. Serve with vegetables like Quick Stewed Eggplant with Coconut (page 152) for a vegetarian meal or along with meat, chicken, or fish. Also feel free to double the batch and freeze any extra breads (wrap them individually in plastic wrap and then store them in an airtight plastic bag), so you can pop a frozen one into the toaster any time you want a homemade flatbread.

MAKES FOUR 6-INCH ROUND BREADS

½ cup whole milk

1 teaspoon active dry yeast

¼ cup plain yogurt

3 tablespoons canola oil, plus more for cooking

1 large carrot, coarsely grated

1 green bell pepper, stemmed, seeded, and finely chopped

2 cups all-purpose flour, plus more as needed

½ teaspoon baking powder

1 teaspoon kosher salt

1 teaspoon granulated sugar

Place the milk in a small saucepan set over low heat and warm just until it reaches body temperature, about 1 minute (or microwave it in 10-second bursts). Pour the milk into a large bowl and stir in the yeast. Let the mixture sit until the yeast has dissolved, about 5 minutes. Stir in the yogurt, 2 tablespoons of the oil, the carrot, and bell pepper. In a separate bowl, whisk together the flour, baking powder, salt, and sugar and then stir the dry ingredients into the wet ingredients.

Transfer the dough to a lightly floured work surface and knead until the dough is soft and elastic, about 5 minutes, adding more flour as needed if the dough is too sticky to knead.

Rub the remaining 1 tablespoon oil over the interior surface of a large clean bowl and transfer the dough to it. Cover the bowl with a clean kitchen towel or plastic wrap and let it sit in a warm spot in your kitchen (the inside of a microwave or the oven—neither of which should be turned on—is a good bet) until the dough is a bit puffy and soft, about 45 minutes.

Punch down the dough in the bowl, transfer it to a flour-sprinkled work surface, then cut it into four equal pieces. Working with one piece of dough at a time, use a floured rolling pin to roll the dough into a ¼-inch-thick oval measuring about 6 inches in diameter. You can also just pat the dough into circles with floured hands.

Line a serving basket or dish with a napkin, then set aside. Set a large cast-iron skillet or other heavy skillet over medium heat and let it warm up for 2 minutes. Working with one piece of rolled-out dough at a time, place the dough in the skillet and cook until bubbles start to form on the surface and the underside is brown, about 2 minutes. Flip the bread and spoon about 2 teaspoons of the oil around the edges of the bread, using a fork or tongs to spin the bread around to coat the edges with oil (you are using the bread almost as a brush to spread the oil evenly over the skillet's surface). Cook the bread until it is browned on the underside, about 2 minutes. Transfer the ajemi to the prepared basket or dish, cover with another napkin, and repeat the process with the remaining pieces of dough, adding a little bit of oil to the skillet as you cook. Serve the ajemi warm. Leftover breads can be stored in a plastic bag at room temperature for a day and rewarmed in a skillet set over low heat before serving (or see the headnote for information about freezing them).

Zanzibar Pilau

(RICE PILAF)

This rice dish is emblematic of all the recipes in this book—the story of the spice trade along the Indian Ocean, the story of Arab settlers in East Africa, and the story of inexpensive ingredients turned into something with so much flavor. Zanzibar, an archipelago off the coast of mainland Tanzania, is home to about a million people. It sits at the heart of the trade routes between East Africa, Europe, and the Middle East, and the cooking in Zanzibar reflects this incredible mix of cultures. The name pilau, just like the term pilaf, derives from the Persian term polow, which is rice mixed with things like spices, nuts, and meat. This dish is also very similar to Bariis (Basmati Rice Pilaf with Raisins, page 87), but is made with coconut milk and without tomato or raisins. If you are vegan, feel free to substitute coconut oil or olive oil for the butter.

SERVES 4

1 cup long-grain white rice (preferably basmati)

2 tablespoons unsalted butter or ghee

1 small yellow onion, finely diced

5 green cardamom pods

One 2-inch piece cinnamon stick

½ teaspoon ground cloves

½ cup full-fat unsweetened coconut milk

1 cup boiling water

1 teaspoon kosher salt

Place the rice in a fine-mesh sieve and rinse with cold tap water, stirring the rice gently with your hands, until the water runs clear, about 1 minute. Place the rinsed rice in a bowl, cover with cold water, and let it soak for at least 10 minutes and up to 30 minutes.

Meanwhile, place the butter in a medium saucepan set over medium-high heat. Once the butter has melted, add the onion and cook, stirring occasionally, until it begins to soften, about 5 minutes. Add the cardamom, cinnamon, and cloves and cook, stirring, until the mixture smells very fragrant, about 1 minute. Stir in the coconut milk, boiling water, and salt. Drain the rice and add it to the pot. Reduce the heat to low, cover, and cook until the rice has absorbed the liquid and is tender, about 15 minutes. Turn off the heat and let the rice sit, covered, for at least 10 minutes before fluffing with a spoon or a fork. Remove and discard the cinnamon and cardamom (if you can find them, they tend to hide—if you can't find them, just warn your guests). Serve the rice immediately, while it's hot. Leftovers can be stored in an airtight container in the refrigerator and rewarmed in a 300°F oven or in a skillet set over low heat.

Matoke with Steamed Spinach

(STEWED PLANTAINS WITH PINK BEANS, BEEF, AND COCONUT MILK)

Matoke, a hearty and quick stew centered on green plantains, is a beautiful one-pot meal that stretches a small amount of meat into something that can feed an entire family. Ma Vicky tells us that "in the United States, we don't have as many types of bananas as we have at home, but we make do. That's why I add some beef and beans and coconut milk to make it more flavorful." She also tells us that in Bukoba, where she comes from, girls learn to peel bananas at a young age (because they're the ones helping out with the food preparation in the kitchen) and know how to do it *fast*. She thinks she has lost her touch, but we disagree. One of the coolest parts of Ma Vicky's matoke is the way she wraps baby spinach in aluminum foil with a little adobo seasoning and butter and steams it directly on top of the stew as it finishes cooking. It gives you an instant side dish with no extra cleanup, and it's wonderfully clever. "In Tanzania, we would wrap greens in banana leaves and steam them on top of whatever we were stewing. We would unwrap the banana leaves and eat the vegetables directly off of them. The flavor is so nice," Ma Vicky says. While the aluminum foil might not be the same, the technique is. If you can't find canned pink beans, feel free to use pinto or kidney beans instead. You could also leave out the steak (and use olive oil on the spinach instead of butter) if you'd prefer a vegan version.

SERVES 4

6 green plantains

3 tablespoons canola oil

1 large red onion, finely diced

2 medium vine-ripened tomatoes, coarsely chopped

¾ pound bone-in shell steak, excess fat trimmed off and discarded, bone cut out and reserved, and meat cut into bite-sized pieces

1 cup full-fat unsweetened coconut milk, plus more as needed

One 15.5-ounce can pink beans, drained and rinsed

Prepare the plantains by first putting on a pair of disposable gloves to keep your hands from getting too sticky while you peel them, then peel, using a paring knife to help you trim the ends and skin. Cut the plantains in half lengthwise and then cut each into quarters crosswise (you'll end up with eight pieces per plantain). Rinse the plantains in cold water to remove excess starch and then drain. Set them aside.

Warm the oil in a large pot set over medium-high heat and add the onion. Cook until just softened, about 5 minutes. Stir in the tomatoes and cook until some of their juice has evaporated, another 2 minutes or so. Add the beef pieces and the reserved bone and cook until the meat is just barely browned on all sides, 5 minutes. Add the plantains and enough fresh, cold water to nearly cover them. Increase the heat to high and bring to a boil, then immediately lower the heat and partially cover the pot; simmer the mixture until the plantains begin to soften, about 10 minutes.

2 teaspoons adobo seasoning (use your favorite brand or a mix of salt and garlic powder; Ma Vicky uses Goya brand)

Kosher salt

Two 5-ounce packages baby spinach

2 tablespoons unsalted butter, cut into small pieces

Add the coconut milk and beans and cook, partially covered, until the plantains change from opaque white to slightly translucent yellow, about 15 minutes. Sprinkle the mixture with 1 teaspoon of the adobo, stir well to combine, and then season to taste with salt.

While the matoke is simmering, place half the spinach on a very large piece of aluminum foil, dot it with the butter, and sprinkle with the remaining 1 teaspoon adobo. Top with the remaining spinach and then wrap everything tightly in the foil to form a large bundle.

Place the spinach bundle directly on top of the matoke and cover the pot tightly. Cook until the spinach is tender (it will shrink significantly) and the matoke is neither too soupy nor too dry, about 7 more minutes. If the matoke is very soupy, just let it boil, uncovered, for an extra couple of minutes; if it's too dry, add a splash more coconut milk or water. Basically, you want each serving to have a little liquid, but you don't want the plantain mixture to be swimming in liquid. Think stew, not soup. How do you know when it's ready? According to Ma Vicky, "You make a decision that it's enough." (A good message to remember for life in general, too.) Leftovers can be stored in an airtight container in the refrigerator for up to a few days and rewarmed in a heavy pot set over low heat (stir while you heat).

Quick Stewed Eggplant with Coconut

This recipe is so quick, easy, affordable, and healthy—the things we all seem to look for these days. It's also very forgiving. Don't have green bell pepper? Throw in a red one. Forgot to check the pot on the stove while you started doing something else? Not the end of the world—the eggplant will just get silkier if it cooks a little longer. Feel free to also throw in some extra vegetables like thinly sliced carrots, chopped okra, or diced sweet potatoes. This is one of those dishes you can throw together after work and just eat with rice or flatbread, or make as part of a more elaborate meal with other vegan dishes (try it with Kunde [Black-Eyed Peas and Tomatoes in Peanut Sauce, page 127]) or meat, chicken, or fish.

SERVES 4

2 pounds eggplant (about 2 large), cut into 2-inch pieces

1 large red onion, finely chopped

1 green bell pepper, stemmed, seeded, and thinly sliced

4 garlic cloves, minced

2 jalapeños, stemmed and thinly sliced (use less or leave out if you don't want things too spicy)

¼ teaspoon ground turmeric

1 teaspoon kosher salt

½ cup full-fat unsweetened coconut milk

Place the eggplant, onion, bell pepper, garlic, jalapeños, turmeric, salt, and coconut milk in a large pot and stir well to combine. Set over high heat and bring to a boil, then reduce the heat to low, cover, and simmer until the eggplant is tender, about 10 minutes. Season the eggplant to taste with salt and serve immediately. Leftovers can be stored in an airtight container in the refrigerator for up to a few days and rewarmed in a heavy pot set over low heat (stir while you heat).

Spiced Fried Fish

Ma Shara's assertive garlic and spice mixture takes fried fish from good-but-plain to unforgettably flavorful. Frying fish might seem intimidating, but working with steaks or fillets instead of whole fish makes it quite easy to handle. Use a heavy pot with tall sides (at least 4 inches tall) to keep yourself protected from any splatters. Serve with lemon or lime wedges for squeezing over, a big pot of Zanzibar Pilau (Rice Pilaf, page 148), and a fresh salad for a wonderful dinner. This fried fish also makes an excellent fish sandwich piled on a bun or flatbread like Ajemi Bread with Carrots and Green Pepper (page 146), topped with shredded cabbage or lettuce.

SERVES 4

5 garlic cloves, minced

1 teaspoon freshly ground black pepper

1 teaspoon ground ginger

1 teaspoon ground cumin

1 tablespoon kosher salt

Four 6-ounce steaks or fillets (firm, oily fish such as kingfish, mackerel, bluefish, tuna, or swordfish)

Canola oil, for frying

Place the garlic, pepper, ginger, cumin, and salt together in a mortar and crush with a pestle until coarsely ground (or just mix together in a bowl—the flavor won't be as intense, but it will still be great). Using your hands, evenly spread the garlic mixture over the fish and let the fish sit at room temperature for 10 minutes while you prepare your oil for frying (or cover the fish and refrigerate for up to 24 hours; take it out of the refrigerator 10 minutes before frying).

Line a plate or tray with paper towels and set aside. Heat 1 inch of oil in a Dutch oven or other heavy pot set over medium-high heat until it reaches 375°F on an instant-read thermometer or until bubbles form around the handle of a wooden spoon (just stick the end of the spoon in the pot to test the temperature). Carefully add the fish to the hot oil, working in batches if necessary, depending on the size of your pot, and cook, turning occasionally, until browned on all sides, about 5 minutes. Transfer the fried fish to the prepared plate or tray to drain. Serve hot.

Harees with Chicken

(STEWED CRACKED WHEAT AND CHICKEN)

A savory porridge made of cracked wheat with meat (we use chicken thighs), harees is a popular Arab dish that was introduced to East Africans by Arab settlers when they first arrived generations ago. It's also commonly known as 'bokoboko' and is regularly enjoyed during Ramadan. It's simple and comforting and can be served as is or topped with fried onions, if you'd like to add some extra flavor and texture.

SERVES 4

1 pound bone-in, skin-on chicken thighs

1 small yellow onion, halved

One 1-inch piece cinnamon stick

3 green cardamom pods

1 tablespoon kosher salt, plus more as needed

6 cups water

¾ cup cracked wheat (sometimes labeled coarse bulgur wheat)

3 tablespoons ghee or unsalted butter, melted

Place the chicken thighs, onion, cinnamon, cardamom, salt, and water in a large Dutch oven or other heavy pot set over high heat. Bring the water to a boil, reduce the heat to low, and simmer until the broth is fragrant and the chicken is tender, about 30 minutes.

Use tongs to transfer the chicken thighs to a plate and let them rest until they're cool enough to handle. Continue to simmer the broth while the chicken thighs cool. Once they're cool, shred the meat and discard the skin and bones. Use a handheld sieve to remove the onion halves, cinnamon, and cardamom from the broth (or strain the broth into a bowl, discard the solids, and then return the broth to the pot). Return the shredded chicken to the broth, add the cracked wheat, and simmer, stirring occasionally, until the wheat is tender and the porridge is thick and creamy, about 45 minutes. Season the porridge to taste with salt and stir in the ghee just before serving. Serve immediately, while hot. Leftovers can be stored in an airtight container for up to a few days and rewarmed in a heavy pot set over low heat before serving (stir while you heat); the mixture will thicken as it cools, so feel free to loosen it with a little extra water or stock when reheating.

Ma Vicky's Famous Lasagna

"When I started making it, my family liked it, so we made it our favorite," Ma Vicky told us about her famous lasagna. Her signature dish includes a couple key elements. One is a highly seasoned spinach mixture that makes up two layers of the lasagna, and the other is a thick layer of tomato sauce she puts on top of the lasagna. While we were curious if Ma Vicky would have Tanzanian-inspired spices in her sauce or in the lasagna layers, we found that it's really a classic Italian American lasagna, the kind of lasagna any grandmother in America might make on a Sunday afternoon. Which is exactly who Ma Vicky is: a woman living in America who cooks regularly for her family. She's also East African, which means her cooking is influenced by a long history of Italian colonization throughout the region, making dishes like lasagna just as familiar as dishes with plantains. Ma Vicky's lasagna is so beloved in her large family that she makes two at a time; this recipe reflects that, but feel free to cut the amounts in half and make just one. But honestly, if you're going to expend the energy, it's best to go ahead and make two. You can always freeze one for later (either freeze it unbaked and bake it directly from the freezer, adding an extra 45 minutes to the baking time, or freeze it baked, defrost in the refrigerator, and then just warm it up in the oven).

SERVES 12

Kosher salt

One 1-pound box uncooked lasagna noodles

4 tablespoons extra-virgin olive oil

3 yellow onions, finely diced

5 garlic cloves, minced

Three 10-ounce packages frozen chopped spinach, thawed

2 chicken or vegetable bouillon cubes

½ cup heavy cream

1 teaspoon adobo seasoning (use your favorite brand or a mix of salt and garlic powder; Ma Vicky uses Goya brand)

8 cups tomato sauce (use your favorite recipe or brand; Ma Vicky's is meat-flavored Prego)

Preheat the oven to 375°F.

Bring a large pot of water to a boil and salt it generously. Add the lasagna noodles and cook, stirring occasionally to keep them separated, until they're just al dente, about 9 minutes. Drain the noodles in a colander, toss them with 1 tablespoon of the oil to keep them from sticking to each other, and set them aside.

Meanwhile, warm the remaining 3 tablespoons oil in a large heavy pot set over medium heat. Add the onion and garlic and cook, stirring occasionally, until softened, about 10 minutes.

Stir in the spinach (with whatever liquid is in the packages), bouillon, cream, and adobo. Bring the mixture to a boil, decrease the heat to maintain a simmer, and cook for just a minute to really imbue the spinach with all the seasoning. Season the spinach to taste with salt. When you taste it to season it, Ma Vicky insists that you transfer a little bit of the mixture from your mixing spoon to your hand rather than taste directly from the spoon ("Only in America!" she says). Set aside the spinach mixture.

1 cup finely grated Parmesan cheese

One 32-ounce container full-fat ricotta cheese

3 cups shredded mozzarella cheese (preferably preshredded, not fresh mozzarella, which contains too much water for lasagna—plus, preshredded is much easier!)

Place two 9 by 13-inch pans on your work surface. Place 1½ cups of the tomato sauce in each pan and spread the sauce with a spoon to cover the bottoms. Place a single, even layer of noodles over the sauce in each pan (each should take about one-sixth of the noodles—you will be making a total of three layers of noodles per pan).

Sprinkle the noodles in each pan evenly with a light layer of the Parmesan cheese (about 2 to 3 tablespoons on each lasagna). Place a quarter of the spinach mixture in each pan (you will have two layers of spinach in each lasagna) and, using a spoon, spread to cover. Place a quarter of the ricotta in each pan (you will have two layers of ricotta in each lasagna) and, using a spoon, spread to cover. Add another layer of noodles over the ricotta and sprinkle them with another light layer of Parmesan cheese (about 2 to 3 tablespoons on each lasagna). Sprinkle each lasagna evenly with ½ cup of the mozzarella, then divide the remaining spinach mixture between the pans and spread to cover. Dollop the remaining ricotta over the spinach layer and sprinkle with a light layer of Parmesan cheese. Top each lasagna with a final layer of noodles and divide the remaining tomato sauce between the lasagnas (it will be a thick layer).

Cover each pan tightly with aluminum foil and bake for 25 minutes. Uncover the lasagnas and evenly sprinkle the tops with the remaining Parmesan and mozzarella cheeses. Return the lasagnas to the oven and bake, uncovered, until the sauce is bubbling and the cheese has melted, another 25 minutes or so. Turn your oven from bake to broil and broil the top of the lasagnas, until the cheese is browned, about 1 minute. Watch carefully to make sure it does not burn.

Let the lasagnas rest at room temperature for 15 minutes, then slice and serve. This lets all the layers set a bit so you don't end up with too-messy slices. Serve immediately. Leftovers can be stored in an airtight container in the refrigerator for up to a few days and rewarmed uncovered in a 350°F oven for about 20 minutes.

Date Bread

This simple quick bread includes tons of juicy Medjool dates, making it an option for breaking the daily sunrise-to-sunset fast during the holy month of Ramadan, a tradition that Muslims observe in Tanzania and across the world. The tradition is rooted in the teachings of the prophet Muhammad, who is said to have called for observers to break their fasts with dates. Many Muslims include dates on their iftar tables (iftar is the evening meal eaten at sunset during Ramadan). This bread can, of course, be enjoyed by any and all, year-round. It's wonderful on its own with hot cups of coffee like Buna (Eritrean Coffee, page 54) or tea like Shaah Cadays (Somali Spiced Tea with Milk, page 94) or topped with a soft cheese like goat cheese, ricotta, or cream cheese. It's also wonderful served in slices on a cheese board. If you can't find Medjool dates, use whichever are the plumpest, least-dry dates you can find or substitute your favorite dried fruit such as dried apricots or dried cherries (you need about 1 cup of your favorite dried fruit).

MAKES ONE 9 BY 5-INCH LOAF

12 Medjool dates, pitted and coarsely chopped

½ teaspoon kosher salt

1 teaspoon baking soda

½ cup boiling water

¼ cup granulated sugar

4 tablespoons unsalted butter, at room temperature

1 large egg

2 teaspoons pure vanilla extract (preferably from Madagascar or Comoros)

2 cups all-purpose flour

Preheat the oven to 350°F. Spray a 9 by 5-inch loaf pan with nonstick spray.

Place the dates in a small bowl and sprinkle with the salt and baking soda. Pour the boiling water over the mixture and allow it to sit until it cools.

Meanwhile, in the bowl of a mixer fitted with the whisk attachment or in a large bowl using a handheld mixer (or a whisk and a lot of elbow grease), beat the sugar and butter until creamy. Add the egg and vanilla and beat until well combined, about 1 minute. Using a rubber spatula, stir in the date mixture (water and all) and then fold in the flour. The batter will be very stiff.

Transfer the batter to the prepared loaf pan and, using a rubber spatula, smooth out the top so the loaf is even. Bake until the loaf is dark golden brown, a toothpick tests clean when inserted into the center of the loaf, and the bread is firm to the touch, about 40 minutes. Let the bread cool completely on a wire rack before turning it out of the pan and slicing it. Leftovers can be stored in a plastic bag at room temperature for up to 3 days (if the slices get a bit dry, you can revive them in a toaster oven or regular oven set at 300°F for a few minutes before serving).

Fresh Mango Juice

Fresh mango juice is served all over the African continent and is a wonderful accompaniment to just about any meal—from breakfast to evening cocktails (just spike it with some rum). Most commercial mango juice is heavily sweetened and more like mango-flavored sugar water. We like ours fresh and bright and flavored with just mango, lime juice, and a tiny bit of salt to bring out the natural flavors. If you prefer yours a bit sweeter, just add a little sugar or honey to the blender. Store any extra juice in the refrigerator for up to 3 days (stir before serving).

SERVES 4

2 mangoes, pitted, peeled, and diced

½ cup freshly squeezed lime juice

2 cups water

½ teaspoon kosher salt

Ice, for serving

Place the mango, lime juice, water, and salt in the jar of a blender and puree until smooth. Fill four glasses with ice and divide the drink among them. Serve immediately.

Kaimati

(CRISPY COCONUT DUMPLINGS IN CARDAMOM SYRUP)

These fried dumplings originated and are popular along what's known as the Swahili coast, which includes the coastal parts not only of Tanzania but also of Zanzibar, Kenya, and northern Mozambique. Kaimati, which are sometimes called dabo or dahir, are commonly flavored with cardamom and coconut but can be made plain without any spices or sugar. Once you start frying, gather your friends and family around to eat them immediately—they're best when fresh and hot.

**MAKES ABOUT
24 DOUGHNUTS**

1¼ cups full-fat unsweetened coconut milk

½ teaspoon active dry yeast

1 cup all-purpose flour

1 cup water

1 cup granulated sugar

2 teaspoons green cardamom pods, gently crushed

1 teaspoon freshly squeezed lemon or lime juice

Canola oil, for frying

Place the coconut milk in a large bowl and stir in the yeast. Let the mixture sit until the yeast has completely dissolved, about 5 minutes. Stir in the flour and, using a wooden spoon or your hand, mix well for about 5 minutes to help develop the gluten in the mixture (the mixture will be a loose dough and mixing it will be more like slapping it against itself rather than kneading). The dough will be thick and sticky. Cover the bowl with a clean kitchen towel or plastic wrap and let the dough sit at room temperature until it's slightly risen, at least 30 minutes and up to 1 hour.

Meanwhile, place the water in a large pot, add the sugar and crushed cardamom, set the pot over high heat, and bring to a boil. Reduce the heat to low and allow the mixture to simmer until it's slightly thickened, about 20 minutes. Turn off the heat, stir in the lemon juice, and allow the mixture to cool to room temperature in the pot.

Heat 1 inch of oil in a Dutch oven or other heavy pot set over medium-high heat until it reaches 375°F on an instant-read thermometer or until a pinch of dough sizzles on contact. Dip your fingers into a bowl of cold water, then

pinch off a tablespoon of dough and shape it as well as you can into a small ball (wetting your fingers will prevent the dough from sticking to them but be careful not to wet your hands so much that water drips into the hot oil). Carefully place the dough ball into the hot oil and repeat the process until you have enough balls to fill the pot, allowing some space between each (probably about six at a time, depending on the size of your pot). Use a slotted spoon to continuously turn and stir the dough balls so they brown evenly; fry until golden brown all over, about 4 minutes. Use the slotted spoon to lift and drain the fried dumplings and carefully transfer them to the syrup. Stir to coat the dumplings in the syrup, then transfer them to a serving dish and repeat the process with the rest of the dough. Serve immediately while they're at their crunchiest.

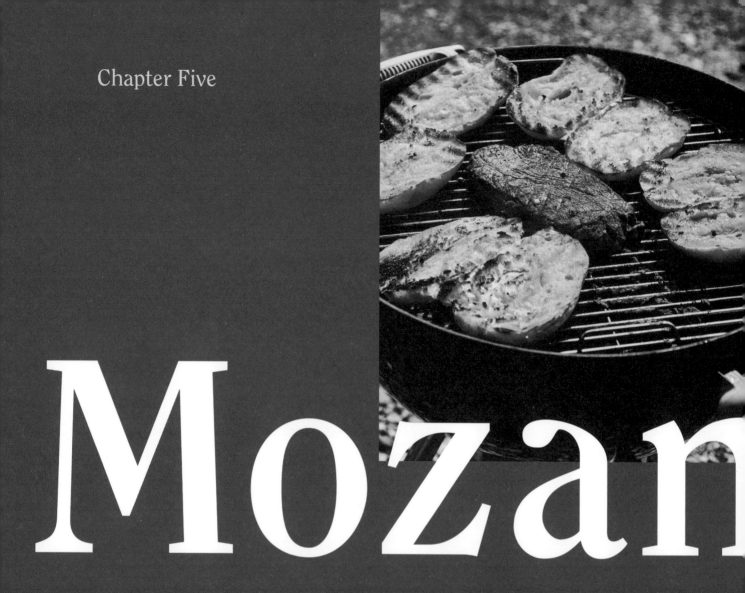

Chapter Five

Mozan

nbique

Mozambique boasts a coastline that stretches about 1,500 miles, at least twice the length of the country's width. People arrived in Mozambique around the first century and immediately started fishing, farming, and raising livestock in small villages that eventually turned into larger kingdoms. These kingdoms remained fairly isolated until the eighth century, when Arabian settlers found their way to Mozambique and established trade networks (remember that long coastline?).

Vasco da Gama, the first European to reach India by sea, stopped at Mozambique Island, a small island attached to Mozambique, along his way to India. Within the next few years, the Portuguese took control of many of the trading posts on the island, and over the next two centuries, they set up tons more trading posts and named the island Portuguese East Africa. In addition to trading gold and ivory, they also traded enslaved Africans, and it's said that almost one million enslaved Africans were sold by way of Mozambique's ports—one of the many lasting effects of Portugal's colonization.

In 1899, a labor law drew a line through Mozambique's population to separate indigenous Mozambicans from non-indigenous ones. Those who were originally from Mozambique were forced to work and were subject to different taxes and laws. Non-indigenous Mozambicans were given full Portuguese citizenship and could forgo many of those extra duties. The People's Republic of Mozambique achieved independence in 1975, and the Portuguese left almost immediately.

For the next decade, Mozambique attempted to implement socialist policies and was plagued with instability. There was a civil war from 1977 until 1992. In 1983, a drought brought famine, and Mozambique sought Western aid. In 1992, a peace agreement was reached within the country, and since then, there has been more stability, although corruption and poor governance continue to plague Mozambique to the present day.

Geography and Climate

Mozambique sits on the southeast coast of Africa. Swaziland is to its south, Tanzania to its north, Zimbabwe to its west, and Zambia and Malawi to its northwest. Its climate is tropical; its northeastern area is prone to monsoons.

Before the city of Maputo became Mozambique's capital, Mozambique Island was the country's capital. The island is full of difficult history—it was a major slave-trading post and drips with colonialism. Although it is very small (barely 2 miles long), it has had a huge impact on so many lives. The island is now a UNESCO World Heritage Site. Maputo, on the other hand, is a modern city that symbolizes Mozambique's liberation.

Economy and Resources

Potential is the key word for Mozambique's economy. Many companies are working on building plants to harness natural gas from the reserves found in the Rovuma Basin, which will eventually make Mozambique one of the world's most significant natural gas producers. Mozambique's coastline, wildlife, and history also make it ripe for increased tourism, attracting travelers seeking everything from beaches to cultural deep dives.

People

Mozambique is home to more than twenty-five million people, and the population consists mostly of sixteen ethnic groups, all of whom derive from the Bantu people. A small percentage of Mozambicans are of Portuguese descent. There is also a large Indian community in Mozambique, as well as a small Chinese community. Most Mozambicans live in the north-central provinces of Nampula and Zambezia.

Language

One of the most lasting effects of the Portuguese in Mozambique is the language. Portuguese continues to be the country's official language and the most widely spoken one, too. In addition, many African languages are spoken, including Changana, Makhuwa, and Swahili.

Religion

Mozambicans practice many traditional religions, most of which are based on animism (the belief that everything, from people to objects, has a spiritual essence and is, in effect, alive). Unsurprisingly for a place so steeped in history, ancestors are held sacred, and the country contains a number of sacred sites and many traditional healers who are highly respected. But many Mozambicans no longer practice traditional religions, turning instead to Christianity (specifically Protestantism), Catholicism, and Islam.

Ma Maria

HOME
Maputo, Mozambique

HER RECIPES
Tseke com Peix Frito (Local Spinach with Curry Sauce and Crispy Fried Fish, page 178)

Coril de Peix com Coco (Marinated Fish in Coconut Sauce, page 179)

Xima (Smooth Cornmeal Porridge, page 182)

Mbowa (Leafy Greens in Coconut Sauce, page 183)

Why did you choose to make the recipes you shared with us?

Because they are typical from Mozambique and I usually cook them at home. It means comfort, and it is what I like to cook. Also, because when I prepare them, I receive a lot of compliments.

What dish best represents Mozambican food?

Fish and coconut milk curry. Greens with coconut milk. Grilled chicken. These represent the local taste, the Mozambican taste.

How often do you cook, and do you enjoy cooking?

Yes, and I like it a lot, too much. I worked as a housekeeper and in a kitchen since 1985. And I learned to cook on the job.

Do your children and grandchildren cook? If so, did you teach them to cook?

Yes, my daughter learned from me. She cooks very well.

What does home mean to you?

Something I like. I like my home. And I think everyone should have theirs.

How do you define community?

A quiet and safe place. I enjoy my own community.

Looking back, what are you most proud of?

My kids and grandsons.

What was your favorite meal growing up? Who made it?

I grew up in a rural area, so the food was pretty basic but always Mozambican. I liked to eat xima and beans. My favorite were indjuvu, a type of bean that needs to be peeled. My mom made them.

Ma Josefina

HOME
Quelimane, Zambezia Province,
Mozambique

HER RECIPE
Plantains with Coconut and Prawns (page 188)

What dish best represents Mozambican food?

Xima [a smooth cornmeal porridge; see Ma Maria's on page 182].
It's eaten everywhere in Mozambique in almost the same way.

What part of the country are you from?

I'm from Quelimane, the capital of the Zambezia Province.
It's at the center.

What dish best represents that area?

It's mucapata. It's a kind of bean, very small beans. They have a green
cover, and we put them in a mortar and press them to take off that cover
and you find the small yellow seeds. We cook them with coconut. All the
dishes in Quelimane are made with coconut. You can have anything eaten
at breakfast with coconut, anything at lunch with coconut, anything
takes coconut! For mucapata, we mix three parts beans with one part
rice, and we boil them until they're cooked, then we drain them and mix
them with coconut milk and then you eat it with chicken.

*Why did you choose to make plantains with prawns to share
with us?*

Because it's easy! [*laughs*] And because I didn't have much time to
prepare something more elaborate, so I chose the easiest thing to do.

I could've done mucapata, but it takes a long time to prepare. Both are traditional, very traditional, dishes from my town, and the bananas with prawns are easier.

How has the food changed in Mozambique?

We invent things now! The way I'm doing these bananas is not the way I learned from my mother. I put onion, I put garlic. My mother wouldn't do that. She would just do banana, coconut, and salt. So, we try to improve, we try to make dishes that we can take and share with other people, and it's nice for the eyes and still maintains the taste. While the traditional way is done in a way that's nice for the taste but doesn't think very much of the appearance. We think a lot about the appearance nowadays. And the majority of the dishes now use oil, and I see many people doing traditional dishes that use coconut but they start with oil and then put the coconut because that's what people are getting used to now. They're not comfortable just using coconut.

So, the tradition is not to use oil?

No, no, we wouldn't use oil at all.

How often do you cook?

I cook every day.

Do you enjoy it?

I do! [*laughs*] I learned it since I was kid, and I do enjoy it. When I don't want to cook, I don't, nowadays—but when I was younger, I had to cook.

Do your children cook?

No, they don't. They can fry an egg, but that's all!

Why don't they cook? They just don't have any interest?

They don't like cooking. They're all boys.

How do you define community?

I think we have many communities. We are part of many communities, different communities. Living here in Maputo, I feel like I belong to a community of people who come from my township. I'm part of a community from my church and a community from where I studied. A group of people who identify themselves by sharing something. They

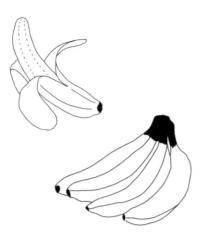

have something in common. They share a background or a religion, or they share a place that they live together, or something they're planning for the future. The same goals and the same objectives make community.

What was your favorite meal growing up?

I think rice and meat, it's always been rice. Now that I'm grown up, I love xima, but when I was younger, I hated xima. But now I like it.

What role has gender played in your community?

In my community growing up, my perception of gender roles was more in my mother's view. I was taught that a woman has to be conservative, that you can't go out in the night, you can't go to nightclubs and all of those things, but boys can do all of those things. My mother was like that, but although when it came to education, she thought we all have to go to school and we all have to study, whether you're a woman or a man. But in terms of the house and all of those things, she was really tough on women, on us, but not much on the boys. In terms of Mozambican society, I think our way of living is that a woman is different from a man, and it doesn't end all in the differences. A man is more than a woman, and as a woman, you have to do much more to conquer the same thing a man can conquer. That's what I think of Mozambique.

Do you think with this new generation that gender roles are changing?

I do think they're changing. Although the society is still dominated by men, women find their way through. I believe sooner or later that things will change. We see some changes, but they're not enough. I remember when I was studying, I had a teacher who would say that talking about feminism was dangerous. It was better to talk about gender because just as women were taught to be at home and take care of kids and all of those things, men were taught to take care of the family, bring the bread, and all of those things. With the growth of women in the economic arena, men lose some space, and they can be shocked. So, we have to think both ways, not only to make sure that women grow economically, but make sure also that there are no disparities that men fall without jobs. That's not what we want; we want a society that works together.

Tseke com Peix Frito

(LOCAL SPINACH WITH CURRY SAUCE AND CRISPY FRIED FISH)

This fish, marinated with garlic and lime and fried in a simple egg-and-flour batter, is served with curry-infused spinach and is a testament to Ma Maria's beautiful way of preparing food that's simple yet layered with flavor. Enjoy this dish with some cooked rice.

SERVES 4

3 garlic cloves, minced

3 tablespoons freshly squeezed lime juice

½ teaspoon kosher salt, plus more as needed

4 small whole mackerel (about 1½ pounds each), cleaned and cut in half crosswise

1 cup all-purpose flour

1 large egg

Canola oil, for frying

1 large yellow onion, thinly sliced

2 medium vine-ripened tomatoes, coarsely chopped

1 teaspoon curry powder or Xawaash Spice Mix (page 74)

1 pound mature (not baby) spinach, coarsely chopped

1 chicken bouillon cube

¼ cup water

Stir together the garlic, lime juice, and salt in a shallow bowl. Add the mackerel and, using your hands, coat the mackerel with the marinade. Set the mackerel aside.

Place the flour on a large plate and the egg in a shallow bowl; beat the egg well with a fork or a whisk. Coat each piece of marinated fish first in the flour (knock off any excess), then in the egg, then in the flour one last time.

Meanwhile, line a plate with paper towels and set aside. Heat 1 inch of oil in a Dutch oven or other heavy pot set over medium-high heat until it reaches 375°F on an instant-read thermometer or until a piece of fish sizzles on contact. Carefully place the fish in the hot oil, working in batches as necessary, depending on the size of your pot, then fry, turning the fish with a slotted spoon as they cook, until they are golden brown all over, about 8 minutes. Carefully transfer the fish to the prepared plate to drain and then sprinkle with a little bit of salt. Set the fish aside.

Carefully transfer 3 tablespoons of the oil you cooked the fish to a separate large pot and set it over medium-high heat. Add the onion and cook, stirring occasionally, until just beginning to soften, about 5 minutes. Add the tomatoes, curry powder, spinach, bouillon, and water to the pot and mix well to combine. Cover and simmer until the spinach is very tender, about 10 minutes. Season the spinach to taste with salt. Transfer the spinach to a serving dish, top with the fried fish, and serve immediately.

Coril de Peix com Coco

(MARINATED FISH IN COCONUT SAUCE)

Just like Ma Maria's Tseke com Peix Frito (Local Spinach with Curry Sauce and Crispy Fried Fish, opposite), this fish dish takes advantage of all the local flavors in Mozambique. Serve with Ma Maria's Xima (Smooth Cornmeal Porridge, page 182) or plain rice to soak up all of the sauce.

SERVES 4

2 large tomatoes

6 garlic cloves, minced

4 small whole mackerel (about 1½ pounds each), cleaned

Canola oil for frying

1 large yellow onion, thinly sliced

1 teaspoon curry powder or Xawaash Spice Mix (page 74)

1 chicken bouillon cube

2 large carrots, coarsely chopped

2 cups full-fat unsweetened coconut milk

1 cup water

2 jalapeños, stemmed and thinly sliced (use less or leave out if you don't want things too spicy)

Kosher salt

Cut off and discard a thin slice from the stem end of each tomato and then coarsely grate the tomatoes on a box grater directly into a bowl. Discard the skins. Set the grated tomatoes aside.

Line a plate with paper towels and set aside. Rub half the minced garlic all over the fish. Heat ½ inch of oil in a large nonstick skillet set over high heat until it reaches 375°F or until a piece of fish sizzles on contact. Carefully add the fish to the skillet and cook, turning once, until dark brown and crisp on both sides, about 4 minutes per side. Transfer the fish to the prepared plate and set aside.

Meanwhile, place the 3 tablespoons oil in a Dutch oven or other large heavy pot set over medium-high heat. Add the onion and cook, stirring occasionally, until beginning to soften, about 5 minutes. Add the remaining minced garlic and cook, stirring, until fragrant, about 30 seconds. Add the grated tomatoes, curry powder, and bouillon. Cook, stirring occasionally, until the mixture is almost dry, about 5 minutes. Add the carrots, coconut milk, and water and bring the mixture to a boil. Reduce the heat to low and stir in the jalapeños. Season the sauce to taste with salt and then add the fish to the sauce. Simmer until the fish has absorbed some of the sauce, about 5 minutes per side. Serve immediately, spooning the sauce over the fish.

Rum with Homemade Berry Soda

Rum is the most popular spirit in Mozambique, and it's usually mixed with a berry-flavored soda. We opted to make our own soda, so it's not too sweet. While we mix the soda with dark rum, per Mozambican tradition, you could substitute tequila, gin, or vodka. You could also skip the rum and substitute sparkling wine for the seltzer, or just leave out the alcohol altogether and just enjoy the soda on its own over ice with a splash of lime or lemon juice.

SERVES 4

One 10-ounce package frozen mixed berries, thawed

¼ cup honey

¼ cup freshly squeezed lemon juice

½ cup dark rum

2 cups seltzer

Ice, for serving

Place the berries (and whatever defrosted juice is in the package with them), honey, and lemon juice in the jar of a blender and puree until smooth. Pour the mixture through a fine-mesh sieve into a pitcher and press down to extract all the flavor from the berries (discard the contents of the sieve). Stir in the rum and seltzer. Fill four glasses with ice and divide the drink among the glasses. Serve immediately.

Xima

(SMOOTH CORNMEAL PORRIDGE)

A staple of Mozambican tables, xima is a smooth porridge made of ground cornmeal, salt, and water. Similar to grits in America and polenta in Italy, xima served with nothing more than a little butter or ghee is a smooth and comforting dish—the perfect thing to warm you up. Ma Maria serves it with her dishes just as she would rice: it absorbs sauces and gravies beautifully.

SERVES 4

5 cups water

1 cup finely ground white cornmeal (see page 18 for more about finely ground white cornmeal)

2 teaspoons kosher salt

Place the water in a medium pot set over high heat and bring to a boil. Reduce the heat to low and slowly whisk in the cornmeal and salt. Cook, stirring regularly with a wooden spoon, until the mixture is thick and creamy and the cornmeal is no longer grainy, about 15 minutes. If the cornmeal gets too thick or too dry, simply add more boiling water. Serve hot. Leftovers can be stored in an airtight container in the refrigerator for up to a few days and rewarmed in a pot set over low heat (stir while you heat and add splashes of water as needed to return the porridge to its original soft texture).

Mbowa

(LEAFY GREENS IN COCONUT SAUCE)

While Ma Maria uses wild pumpkin leaves in this dish (which are readily available in Mozambique), any dark leafy green will do. We like a mix of mature spinach and thinly sliced collard greens. A rich yet totally vegan side dish, these greens complement just about any meal, whether it's a simple bowl of Xima (Smooth Cornmeal Porridge, page 182) or roast chicken.

SERVES 4

3 tablespoons canola oil

2 small yellow onions, thinly sliced

2 medium vine-ripened tomatoes, coarsely chopped

1½ cups full-fat unsweetened coconut milk

1 cup water

½ pound mature (not baby) spinach, coarsely chopped

½ pound dark leafy greens (like collards or kale), tough stems discarded, leaves thinly sliced

Kosher salt

Warm the oil in a large Dutch oven or other heavy pot set over medium heat. Add the onion and cook, stirring occasionally, until just beginning to soften, about 5 minutes. Add the tomatoes and cook just until fragrant and hot, about 1 minute. Add the coconut milk and water and bring the mixture to a boil. Reduce the heat to low and add the spinach and greens in large handfuls, seasoning each handful with a pinch of salt as you add it to the pot (this helps to distribute the salt evenly). Cover and simmer until the greens collapse and begin to become tender, about 5 minutes. Uncover the pot and stir everything well to combine. Simmer, uncovered, until the greens lose their brightness and become extremely tender, another 10 minutes. Season the greens to taste with salt. Serve hot. Leftovers can be stored in an airtight container in the refrigerator for up to a few days and rewarmed in a pot set over low heat (stir while you heat).

Piri Piri Sauce

It's hard to go a day in Mozambique without eating something that's touched with piri piri sauce (sometimes written as peri peri). The sauce, made with chiles, citrus, and oil, is Portuguese in origin, but *peri* is actually the Swahili word for "chile" and refers to a specific type of chile pepper that is said to have been first cultivated in Africa. While the sauce is traditionally made with piri piri chiles, all different kinds of hot peppers work well. We found that red Fresno chiles, readily available in the United States and not quite as hot as jalapeños, work really well. However, if you can only find jalapeños, just use three fresh ones in place of the red Fresno chiles. Use the sauce anywhere you would use sriracha. Try it on grilled chicken, toss it with raw cashews and then roast them for a great snack with cocktails, stir it into a seafood stew, or use it for Prego Rolls (Steak and Piri Piri Sandwiches, page 186).

MAKES ABOUT 1½ CUPS

10 red Fresno chiles, stemmed, seeded, and coarsely chopped

2 garlic cloves, minced

2 tablespoons minced ginger

½ cup freshly squeezed lime juice

¼ cup extra-virgin olive oil

1 tablespoon granulated sugar, plus more as needed

1 teaspoon kosher salt, plus more as needed

In the jar of a blender, combine the chiles, garlic, ginger, lime juice, oil, sugar, and salt and puree until smooth. Season to taste with more salt or sugar if you'd like. Transfer to a jar and store, covered, in the refrigerator for up to 2 weeks.

Prego Rolls

(STEAK AND PIRI PIRI SANDWICHES)

These sandwiches are best made by grilling the steak outside, but you can still make this recipe if you don't have an outdoor grill. Just cook the steak in a ripping-hot cast-iron pan (turn on your exhaust fan and open your windows!). Look for Portuguese rolls at your local grocery store (they're usually near the kaiser rolls), and if you can't find them, a soft bread roll like a ciabatta roll or other flour-dusted roll will work well.

SERVES 4

1 pound skirt steak or flank steak, trimmed of excess fat

1 cup Piri Piri Sauce (page 185)

4 tablespoons unsalted butter, melted

4 garlic cloves, minced

Pinch of kosher salt

4 Portuguese rolls, halved horizontally

Place the steak and ½ cup of the Piri Piri Sauce in a large resealable plastic bag. Using your hands, rub the sauce all over the steak and then seal the bag. Allow the steak to marinate for as little as 15 minutes at room temperature or put it in the refrigerator and let it marinate for up to 24 hours.

When you're ready to grill the steak, prepare an outdoor grill (charcoal or gas, whatever you've got) for medium heat. Remove the steak from the marinade (let any excess drip back in the bag and then discard the bag) and place it on the grill. Grill the steak, turning it every so often, until charred in spots and cooked to your liking (about 3 minutes per side for medium-rare). Transfer the steak to a cutting board and allow it to rest for 10 minutes. Keep your grill on for your rolls.

While the steak is resting, mix the melted butter, garlic, and salt together in a small bowl. Spoon the garlic butter over the cut sides of the rolls and grill them on their cut sides until golden brown, about 1 minute. Transfer the rolls to a serving platter, cut-sides up.

Thinly slice the rested steak and divide it among the bottom halves of the rolls. Drizzle each portion with 2 tablespoons of the Piri Piri Sauce (use up the remaining ½ cup) and close the sandwiches with the top halves of the rolls. Serve immediately.

Plantains with Coconut and Prawns

"Coconut is one of the most important ingredients in our food," Ma Josefina told us in her kitchen, as she squeezed handful after handful of grated coconut mixed with hot water to make her own coconut milk. The coconut milk would soon be poured over plantains she had cut into thick coins, plus some chopped onion and prawns. Simmered together, this simple dish is something her mother used to make for her and her seven siblings. "It's a dish that we used to eat at home. You can have it for breakfast, for lunch, for dinner," she told us. It stretches a small amount of prawns (you can substitute large shrimp) into a dish that can feed a big family. She used about a dozen small green plantains, a variety that we can't find here, so we call for four green plantains, since the ones here are larger. Serve with cooked rice and feel free to top with a little chopped cilantro and/or thinly sliced hot chile peppers, plus some lime wedges for squeezing over.

SERVES 4

4 large green plantains

Two 13-ounce cans full-fat unsweetened coconut milk

1 small yellow onion, finely chopped

3 garlic cloves, minced

1 teaspoon kosher salt, plus more as needed

½ pound uncooked prawns or large shrimp, peeled, deveined, and cut in half crosswise

Prepare the plantains by first putting on a pair of disposable gloves to keep your hands from getting too sticky while you peel them. Using a paring knife to help you trim the ends and skins, peel the plantains. Cut the plantains into 1-inch-thick coins and place them in a bowl of cold water (this will help them release some of their starch). Drain the plantains and place them in a large heavy pot. Stir in the coconut milk, onion, garlic, and salt. Add enough water so the liquid just covers the plantains (it will take 2 cups or so, depending on the size of your pot). Set the pot over high heat and bring the mixture to a boil. Reduce the heat to low and stir in the prawns. Place a lid on the pot but leave it slightly ajar (so steam can escape and the liquid does not boil over) and simmer until the plantains are tender when pierced with a paring knife, about 10 minutes. "When the banana is done, it's done," says Ma Josefina. Season to taste with salt and serve immediately.

Bolo Polana

(CASHEW AND POTATO CAKE)

A popular Mozambican dessert, this cake features ground cashews (local to Mozambique) and cooked potatoes (used in some Portuguese baked goods), both of which come together to make an undeniably decadent cake. *Bolo* means "cake" in Portuguese, and Polana is the name of a neighborhood in Mozambique's capital city, Maputo. Don't skip the orange zest and juice and the vanilla in this recipe—they're essential for balancing the richness of the cashews and potatoes in the batter. This cake is regularly served for special occasions.

SERVES 10

1 large baking potato, peeled and coarsely chopped

1 cup raw cashews

¾ cup unsalted butter, at room temperature

1½ cups granulated sugar

4 large eggs, separated

Finely grated zest and juice of 1 orange

2 teaspoons pure vanilla extract (preferably from Madagascar or Comoros)

½ teaspoon kosher salt

¼ cup heavy cream, half-and-half, or whole milk

1½ cups all-purpose flour

Confectioners' sugar, for serving

Preheat the oven to 350°F. Spray an 8-inch square baking pan with nonstick spray.

Place the potato in a small saucepan and cover with cold water. Set the saucepan over high heat and bring the water to a boil. Lower the heat to maintain a simmer and cook until the potato is tender, about 20 minutes. Drain the potato and mash the flesh with a potato masher until smooth. Set the potato aside.

Place the cashews in the bowl of a food processor and pulse until finely ground. Set the cashews aside.

Meanwhile, in the bowl of a stand mixer fitted with the whisk attachment or in a large bowl using a handheld mixer (or a whisk and a lot of elbow grease), combine the butter and granulated sugar and beat until fluffy. Add the egg yolks, one at a time, whisking until each is incorporated before adding the next. Whisk in the cashews, orange zest, orange juice, vanilla, salt, and cream. Using a rubber spatula, stir the mixture to make sure everything is well combined and then gently fold in the flour and mashed potato.

CONTINUED

Bolo Polana

CONTINUED

Clean the mixer bowl and whisk attachment, return them to the mixer, and whisk the egg whites until they form stiff peaks (or clean your handheld mixer beaters and use those to beat the egg whites in a large bowl). With your rubber spatula, stir a third of the egg whites into the batter to loosen the batter, then gently fold in the remaining egg whites. Transfer the batter to the prepared pan.

Bake the cake until it is golden brown, a toothpick tests clean when inserted into the center of the cake, and the top is firm to the touch, about 1 hour 10 minutes. Let the cake cool completely in the pan on a wire rack. Turn the cake out of the pan and set it right-side up on a serving plate. Dust liberally with the confectioners' sugar, then cut into wedges and serve. Leftover cake can be wrapped tightly in plastic wrap and stored at room temperature for up to a few days.

Chapter Six

South

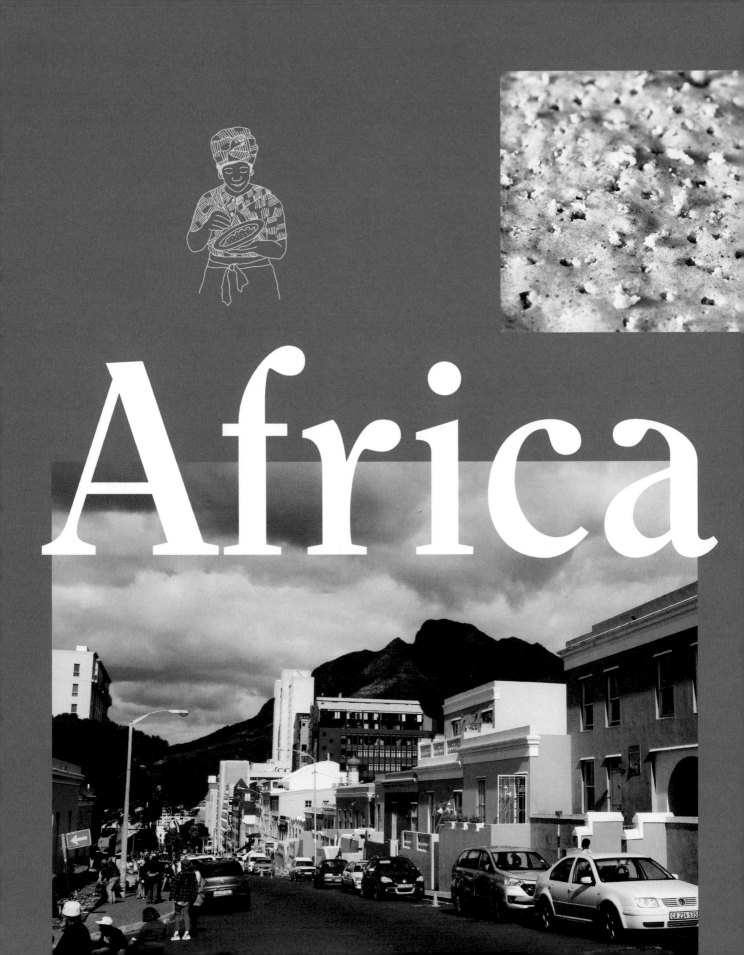

Africa

If you look at the range of cultures that influence food in South Africa, you can get a good sense of the diverse and complicated history of the country. South Africa's indigenous people, the Sotho and the Nguni, have kept a foothold in the country for a long time, and their knowledge of and appreciation for indigenous ingredients like wild plants and game have impacted South African cooking. Many European countries (including the Dutch, German, French, and British, starting in the seventeenth century) colonized South Africa over the years, bringing with them different customs and dishes like German sausages and French jams. In addition to these ingredients, these colonizers also brought people with them. Enslaved Indonesians brought from the Dutch East Indies eventually became their own community, now known as the Cape Malay. Their lasting influence on South African cuisine is evident in the use of ingredients such as tamarind in dishes like Denningvleis (Sweet-and-Sour Braised Lamb with Tamarind, page 208).

The most significant change in the recent history of South Africa is the enfranchisement of black South Africans. Apartheid started in 1948, and it institutionalized segregation and discrimination. Repeal of apartheid began in the 1980s, and black South Africans were finally enfranchised in 1994. Since then, South Africa has sometimes been called the rainbow nation as a way of describing its diverse multicultural society. It is now a liberal democracy, but economic inequality and poverty continue to persist.

Geography and Climate

South Africa is geographically the 25th largest country in the world, is home to over fifty-seven million people, and is the southernmost country on the African continent. It has a long coastline that touches both the Indian Ocean and the South Atlantic Ocean. It sits south of Namibia, Botswana, and Zimbabwe and just southeast of Mozambique. Lesotho, a small country, sits right in the middle of South Africa. The interior of South Africa is mostly flat plateaus, and there's also a long coastline and many mountains. Since it's a subtropical country, most of the country enjoys sunny, warm weather.

Economy and Resources

South Africa has the second-largest economy in Africa (the first is Nigeria), even though it also has very high rates of poverty. Tourism is one of South Africa's driving economic forces. South Africa is rich in a variety of minerals: in addition to diamonds and gold, the country also contains reserves of iron ore, platinum, manganese, chromium, copper, uranium, silver, beryllium, and titanium.

People

Over three-quarters of South Africans are of Bantu ancestry. The remaining descend from European, Indian, and other ancestry.

Language

There are eleven official languages in South Africa, but the four that are most spoken are Zulu, Xhosa, Afrikaans, and English (the other official languages are Tswana, Tsonga, Northern Sotho and Southern Sotho, Swazi, Venda, and Southern Ndebele). Only three other countries in the entire world have more official languages than South Africa.

Religion

The majority of South Africans practice Christianity, but there are small Muslim and Hindu populations and a fairly large Jewish population, too. A number of South Africans practice traditional African religions, and there are hundreds of thousands of indigenous healers, known as sangomas or inyangas. Lots of South Africans consult with these healers.

Ma Khanyisa

HOME
Cape Town, South Africa

HER RECIPE
Imifino (Wild Greens with Corn Porridge, page 211)

Why did you choose to make imifino to share with us, and what does it mean to you?

One, it's easy to make. I also love it because each time I cook it, there is a reminder of home and my childhood when I was growing up. Even when I eat imifino alone, there is always the reminder of community, of women coming together, of sharing not just the food but also sharing themselves. It is really a connection to my childhood, to be honest with you. It's also quite nutritious. The origins of imifino weren't with grown vegetables, but more with wild vegetables, and women had a way of spotting the good ones. As we migrated to cities, we had to find a way to continue the tradition but using vegetables you purchase. Every culture is dynamic, so there are some additions and things we use now to make it more palatable for the table.

What dish best represents South African food?

South Africa is represented by the diversity of the people who are here. We have eleven languages. It's very likely that we have more dishes that we make that represent these many different communities and cultures. It's so funny, because imifino cuts across most African cultures and tribal groups. What's at the core of this are maize meals. South Africans are also meat lovers. If you are a South African, you eat meat. We don't do vegetarianism. We are meat people. We are food people.

What is most misunderstood about South Africa?

People have this thing that we are under siege, that there is always war going on. This is an amazing country with great people who care. I think we are misunderstood to be a violent country. It's not just South Africa. There's a perception that if you come from Africa, you are poor, you are uneducated, and therefore somebody has to make sure you are civilized, and they take it upon themselves to feel sorry for us.

That is true.

Many people don't know where to place South Africa. They don't know if it's a first-class country, a second-class country, a third-world country. People struggle with understanding. There's so much diversity here. We have poverty, and we have disease, but we also have first-world hospitals, and people from Europe come here to have operations. Also, our history of apartheid to some extent placed us differently compared to other African countries. But when you get here, you find things you find in every other country. There are poor people in New York. There's poverty everywhere.

How often do you cook?

I love cooking and I think when you get older, most of the things you like to do, you do them when you feel like doing them. It shifted from cooking for the family because I had to cook for my children and my former husband, to now I still love to cook, but there has to be something that drives me. I still do cook, and when my girls come to visit, they make a special request, and my son, too. "Can I have this when I come?" The one thing I didn't do was teach my children to cook. When you raise children by yourself, there's no time for fun stuff. You get in your routine. There are things they can make for themselves, but they don't know how to make the traditional things.

What does passing on food traditions mean to you?

It's very important because food is part of your identity wherever you are. I'm sure for your country, there are certain foods that you'd feel incomplete if you didn't have them. Food is a big component. It's just like language. For me, stopping traditions would almost be like throwing my culture away, so to speak. That's something that concerns us as our kids become global citizens. The great thing now with healthy eating is that people are going back to how we started, which is good. My mission at the moment, as much as I never really had the chance to teach my girls, is that there are certain foods that I cook when my grandchildren come. So, there are some foods they can identify when they come to Gogo's [what her grandchildren call her] house. It's very important that I keep those traditions.

What does home mean to you?

We always confuse people who are born in the cities when we say we're "going home," but we don't mean to a house. For us, home is where your umbilical cord was buried, because when it fell off when you were five or seven days old when you were a baby, it was buried. So, someone might say, "Where are you from? Where is your umbilical cord buried?" Home for me is where my umbilical cord was buried; it's where everything started, where I was raised, and where my values were shaped to be the woman I am at the moment. So that's home. It is where the people who love you dearly, whose mission it was to shape you into a good citizen, are.

The umbilical cord is so symbolic.

Yes, it is. I've had this property, I've had others in my life, but I've never referred to them as home. And even if it is home for my children because they grew up here, it is not home for me. Home is a place where you feel you can be vulnerable. Where you feel like you can be a child. Home is where I let go of these expectations that I place on myself and that others place on me. It is where I feel like I have arrived, and I am home.

How do you define community?

Community is a place, a setting, where people who love you and who love each other converge with a common purpose and a common vision. We have different communities. We have a community of single moms. We have a community of expats. And each is defined by a common cause.

Looking back, what are you most proud of?

I have so many things that I am proud of. I am incredibly proud of not achievement, per se, but I am proud of having been born in a rural village because it really shaped me to be a caring citizen. Therefore, the achievements that I have made raising my own children single-handedly, traveling around the world meeting incredible people, the things I have achieved academically—I attribute my ability to do all of that to my upbringing in a village with many people who influenced me in many different ways. The whole thing was about raising strong women and caring people, which is very rare these days. People are strong, but they're not always caring. I am proud of how I have become and how I have raised these incredibly feisty and bright and loving and caring and beautiful individuals with their beautiful children. And I attribute it all to my humble beginnings and to my parents, who had no education but who had incredible wisdom. I always think about the coaches we have these days, and my parents never had coaching, but they practiced it.

And by coaching you mean kind of like what you're doing now, mentoring people and assisting young folks and making sure people are guided in the right way?

Yes.

What was your favorite meal growing up?

Imifino. My mom made it. Also, it was a nice in-between meal. And it was usually ready when I got home from school. It was hearty and quick

and nutritious and cooked by someone I loved. I could almost feel my mom, even when she wasn't there after school, if the imifino was there. And we felt that again when she died. A home without a mom is cold. Sometimes when you come from school, you want to tell her something, and she's not there. I am not sure how you [Hawa] did all of that without your mom. When I visit and am sitting in your apartment in New York, I will be asking you these questions!

I will be ready. In your community, are there any gender roles? One thing that stood out to me when I was living in Johannesburg was the mining culture. It felt like the city was full of men and then the outskirts were where women worked, either selling fruit or working at restaurants, stuff like that. Are those gender roles still the same?

Yes, huge, and I think it's going to be that way for probably a very long time. I think one of the things that you probably noticed when you were here is that the people who would stand at traffic lights waiting for work were men; you never saw women. So, they would have been waiting for labor work. Women don't stand. They go knocking on people's doors asking to work, whether to clean their houses or do this or that. Women always make a way. That is still very big in South Africa, especially in our own tribal groupings as well. You almost always see it when you have an event or function or traditional ceremony. That's when you see classically what the role of men is. The role is to set the fire, to slaughter the animal, to get it ready. The role of women is to cook it, to dish it. When there is a funeral, their role is to dig the grave. Our role is to cook for them so when they come back, they eat and get to revive and refresh.

You moved to Australia to study with your ex-husband, and you and your kids lived there for quite some time. Can you tell us what brought you back home? Did you feel like an outsider in Australia?

Well, it's a first-world country, and it has its own culture and cultures within it. It is a Western way of living. As much as those things were not much of a big culture shock since I was coming from Cape Town, which is a city similar to Melbourne, Australia is Australia and South Africa is South Africa. When it was time for me to come back, there was never a question about coming back, especially for myself, because my girls were much younger and had assimilated to Australian culture very quickly. As much as I had friends, and they were all very lovely, I never felt at home. I found the connections very superficial, but here I call it home because that's what it is, *home*. My heart was here. My everything

was here. My family was here. So, I could not stay there as I was. So as much as the girls would've loved to stay, we had to come back. At the same time, I also noticed a trend that since it was a first-world country with everything available, it has the potential to make people less ambitious because you know that you don't have to struggle to take care of yourself. The government will always be there for you during your times of need. I am all for social security, don't get me wrong. But I think even here in South Africa, we are not pushing people to do things for themselves, to become independent. So, it's a dynamic we're also struggling with here. Because it's not in our African makeup. Africans are people who make things happen. It's an inherent thing in us. There's a term called *zenzele*, and it means "do it yourself." So back in the day, that's what we knew. But even when you do the zenzele thing, you do it in a community. People support you. If you have a piece of land, people will come, and you will plow together, you harvest together. It becomes a team thing all the time. There's always support in villages. When you come to the big cities, that's when we start to behave in ways that are un-African, in ways that are cold and distant and not caring for one another. Ubuntu here is lacking [*ubuntu* is a Nguni Bantu term that means "humanity"].

Ubuntu sounds like community. Like closeness to one another.

Yes, yes. It's the saying you are because we are, I am because we are. And it's lacking in a way.

What was the effect of apartheid on people from your tribe?

I think apartheid really destroyed the core of the social fabric of, let me say, Black people, because we're all affected by apartheid in one way or another. Men from rural areas had to leave their families to go in search of work, and some of them never came back; others died, some married other people. So, the women were left to fend for themselves and to raise families and take care of the household. Ubuntu, which is really a core thing that kept us together during apartheid, almost fizzled out. And now it's every man for himself.

It's sad to hear.

Yes, but we're doing the best we can. I was talking to other women about this and, with everything going on, not just apartheid but also globalization and the advancement of technology, we've lost a lot along the way. Some of us are quite conscious of what needs to be repaired, and others are unable to be and don't have the luxury. We're not losing hope; we're doing the best we can. I do have a feeling that this is a phase that will pass at some point. Every war situation does come to an end. You can never have war for the rest of our lives. But at the moment, we have a silent war. We're not physically fighting, but deep under the water, there's a lot of sadness and unhappiness and pain that's going on in the country. And these are the wounds that I think we covered up in 1994, and we got carried away in our euphoria and having a new government. We had the Truth and Reconciliation Commission. But I think that really just scratched the surface. I am all for moving on, but some people are unable to move forward. Especially if they cannot feel a direct link. Apartheid is affecting generations and generations. You do not need to have been there at the time. The impact has gone so deep into other generations.

And we see it from the outside.

It's difficult for people who are outsiders who come in to see some of the goodness of what's going on because people can say, "Oh, you've been out of this for twenty-five years, you cannot continue to call yourselves a country in transition." But the bottom line is that we are still in transition, and it does not justify the mismanagement and corruption. When you dig deeper and look at what's going on, the looting is not just government. Corporations here are looting and misleading. They are just as corrupt because we inherited a corrupt system. But it was glorified as if it was the grandest. But we don't want to lose hope. We just feel this is home for us. And home is home. Look, you still have people living in the Middle East in countries under siege, and you ask yourself, "How do they live?" But people don't understand that there is that thing called home. Yes, you can go now to Canada, but how will you deal with this or that? Even in America, there is still huge racism going on, and they have been liberated for how long? There's still discrimination there. Black people still don't have access to stuff. So, it is a global problem. But all of these things are so entrenched in the system and some of them are so institutionalized that uprooting them, you would really need to have magic people that you are working with. The level of greed at the moment is frightening. Everybody now no longer wants to be in office so that they can make a difference. It's about, "What can I get for myself in this short space of time?"

Chakalaka

(SPICY VEGETABLE RELISH)

Like chutney in India or salsa in Mexico, no one in South Africa prepares chakalaka, a spicy vegetable relish, the same way. And if you ask anyone who makes the best version, they will likely name their own mother or grandmother. Here is our version, full of vegetables and spices. It's akin to giardiniera (the Italian mix of pickled vegetables that includes cauliflower and carrots) and also to English piccalilli relish, whose roots are in South Asian pickled vegetables, which is to say that cultures all across the world have some version of preserved vegetables that enhance many meals. Serve the chakalaka with bread, rice, grilled meats or fish, stews . . . anything. It's particularly delicious with grilled sausages or tucked into a grilled cheese sandwich (see page 210).

MAKES ABOUT 6 CUPS

2 tablespoons canola oil

1 small yellow onion, finely diced

2 garlic cloves, minced

1 jalapeño, stemmed and minced

1 tablespoon minced ginger

2 teaspoons ground turmeric

1 teaspoon ground cumin

1 teaspoon ground coriander

1 teaspoon kosher salt, plus more as needed

1 small red bell pepper, stemmed, seeded, and finely diced

1 small yellow bell pepper, stemmed, seeded, and finely diced

3 large carrots, coarsely grated

½ small green cabbage, finely chopped (about 3 cups)

One 28-ounce can crushed tomatoes

2 tablespoons white vinegar or freshly squeezed lemon juice

Warm the oil in a large Dutch oven or other heavy pot set over medium heat. Stir in the onion, garlic, jalapeño, and ginger. Cook, stirring occasionally, until the onion begins to soften, about 5 minutes. Add the turmeric, cumin, coriander, and salt. Cook, stirring, just until the spices are wonderfully fragrant, about 30 seconds. Stir in the bell peppers, carrots, cabbage, and tomatoes. Reduce the heat to medium-low and cook, uncovered, giving the mixture a stir every so often, until all the vegetables are tender and most of the liquid has evaporated, about 30 minutes. Turn off the heat, stir in the vinegar, and season the chakalaka to taste with salt. Let the chakalaka cool to room temperature and season it to taste one final time. Serve immediately or store in an airtight container in the refrigerator for up to a week, then serve it either cold or at room temperature.

Denningvleis

(SWEET-AND-SOUR BRAISED LAMB WITH TAMARIND)

The tamarind and other dominant flavors in this braised lamb come from the Cape Malay community (see page 195 for more information). If you can't find tamarind paste, you can substitute an equal amount of sherry vinegar or fresh lemon juice in the stew. The taste won't be *exactly* the same, but you will get the nice sweet-and-sour effect along with the brown sugar. Serve with cooked rice and a vegetable such as Sukuma Wiki (Greens with Tomatoes, page 121). You can make this stew up to a week in advance. Just refrigerate it in an airtight container and rewarm it in a pot set over low heat before serving. It's actually one of those dishes that's even better if you make it ahead.

SERVES 4

1 tablespoon canola oil

2 pounds lamb stew meat, preferably with bones, cut into 2-inch pieces (it's best to have your butcher do this so they can cut through the bones)

1 teaspoon kosher salt, plus more as needed

1 large yellow onion, finely diced

2 garlic cloves, minced

2 bay leaves

4 whole cloves

½ teaspoon ground allspice

½ teaspoon ground nutmeg

3 tablespoons tamarind paste

2 tablespoons light brown sugar

⅔ cup water

Preheat the oven to 300°F.

Warm the oil in a large Dutch oven or other heavy ovenproof pot set over medium heat. Season the lamb generously with salt and cook in the oil, in batches as necessary, until browned on all sides, about 10 minutes per batch. Use a slotted spoon to transfer the browned lamb to a plate and set it aside. Once all the lamb is browned, add the onion and garlic to the empty pot and cook, stirring occasionally, until beginning to soften, about 5 minutes. Add the bay leaves, cloves, allspice, nutmeg, tamarind paste, sugar, and water to the pot and stir well to combine. Return the lamb (and whatever juices have collected on the plate) to the pot and stir well to combine. Cover the pot and place it in the oven. Cook until the meat is wonderfully tender, about 1½ hours. Be sure to uncover the pot and give the mixture a stir halfway through the cooking time. Season the lamb to taste with salt and serve hot.

Chakalaka and Cheddar Braaibroodjies

(GRILLED CHEESE SANDWICH)

These grilled cheese sandwiches are typically truly *grilled*, meaning they are thrown on an outdoor grill over open coals, and are usually served as a sort of snack after a big barbecue (known as a braai in South Africa). They're a perfect midnight snack and the best way to make use of still-hot coals if you get a second wave of hunger after you've eaten a meal and the party is still going. The liberal spoonful of Chakalaka (Spicy Vegetable Relish) makes these extra special. If you don't have a jar of it in your fridge, you can use any type of relish or chutney. Since we don't want you to have to wait until you have an outdoor grill going just to make these, we simply call for a hot cast-iron pan. The mayonnaise spread on the outside of the sandwiches means every single bit of the bread will get browned and caramelized (remember, mayonnaise is basically just oil).

MAKES 1 SANDWICH
(EASILY MULTIPLIED)

2 tablespoons mayonnaise

2 slices good-quality sandwich bread

¼ cup grated sharp white Cheddar cheese

¼ cup Chakalaka (Spicy Vegetable Relish, page 207) or any relish or chutney of your choice

2 thin slices onion (any type)

Set a cast-iron pan or other heavy skillet over medium-high heat. Spread 1 tablespoon of the mayonnaise on one side of each slice of bread. Place one slice of bread mayonnaise-side down in the skillet and top it with half the cheese, then top with the chakalaka and onion. Sprinkle the remaining cheese on top of the onion, then place the second piece of bread, mayonnaise-side up, on top. Cover the pan and cook until the bottom of the sandwich is browned, about 2 minutes. Give the sandwich a good press with a spatula and then carefully flip it over, cover, and cook until the second side is browned and the cheese has melted, about 2 minutes. Serve immediately.

MA KHANYISA'S

Imifino

(WILD GREENS WITH CORN PORRIDGE)

Imifino is a word in the Xhosa and Zulu languages that translates to "leafy greens" and usually refers to greens that grow wild. Imifino also refers to a cooked meal of those greens, typically with some onions and seasonings, and served with corn porridge. It's also Ma Khanyisa's favorite food from childhood. "It's a traditional dish usually eaten by women," Ma Khanyisa told us. "For some reason, back in the day, men were not aware of the nutritional value of green vegetables, and they didn't eat them because there was a myth that they made [men] weak. So that might be why African women are so strong—we've always had these traditional meals for ourselves and our children." A healthy, affordable, filling meal, imifino is eaten throughout South Africa. Many older women are passionate about teaching younger generations to identify the greens that grow wild throughout South Africa, whether they're poking out from cracks in the pavement or in fields, so that everyone will always be able to access nutritious food. Ma Khanyisa now makes her imifino with cultivated vegetables and says any mixture of green vegetables works well. Serve it on its own as a meal or a snack, alongside other vegetables or cooked meat, or topped with a fried egg. If you enjoy extra spice, sprinkle it with dried chile flakes, pickled chiles, or a few dashes of hot sauce.

SERVES 4

2½ cups water

½ cup finely ground white or yellow cornmeal

1 teaspoon kosher salt, plus more as needed

3 tablespoons extra-virgin olive oil

1 large yellow onion, finely chopped

2 garlic cloves, minced

1 jalapeño, stemmed and minced

1 small green cabbage, finely chopped (about 6 cups)

2 large or 4 small zucchini, cut into ½-inch-thick slices

One 5-ounce package baby spinach

Place the water in a medium pot set over high heat and bring to a boil. Reduce the heat to low and slowly whisk in the cornmeal and salt. Cook, stirring regularly with a wooden spoon, until the mixture is thick and creamy and the cornmeal is no longer grainy, about 15 minutes. If the mixture gets too thick or too dry, simply add more boiling water. Set the cornmeal aside.

Meanwhile, place the oil in a large Dutch oven or other heavy pot set over medium heat. Add the onion and cook, stirring occasionally, until just beginning to soften, about 5 minutes. Add the garlic and jalapeño and stir just until they sizzle, about 30 seconds. Add the cabbage, zucchini, and spinach and season with a large pinch of salt. Cover and cook, uncovering to stir occasionally, until the vegetables are softened and just tender, about 15 minutes. Transfer the porridge to the pot with the vegetables and mix everything well to combine. Season one final time to taste with salt and serve immediately.

Malva Pudding Cake

Similar to a tres leches cake, this sweet dessert consists of a spongy cake, flavored with apricot jam and cloves, that gets saturated with a syrupy mixture of evaporated milk, brown sugar, and butter while still warm from the oven. Hugely popular throughout South Africa, malva pudding cake became more widely known outside of the country when Art Smith, the celebrity chef who used to cook for Oprah Winfrey, served it for the students of the Oprah Winfrey Leadership Academy for Girls in South Africa following Christmas dinner in 2006.

SERVES 12

Cake

1½ cups all-purpose flour

1 teaspoon baking powder

½ teaspoon kosher salt

½ teaspoon ground cloves

2 large eggs

½ cup granulated sugar

½ cup apricot jam

¾ cup whole milk

Sauce

¾ cup evaporated milk

½ cup firmly packed light brown sugar

4 tablespoons unsalted butter

2 teaspoons pure vanilla extract (preferably from Madagascar or Comoros)

½ teaspoon kosher salt

Make the cake: Preheat the oven to 350°F. Spray an 8-inch square baking pan with nonstick spray.

Place the flour, baking powder, salt, and cloves in a large bowl and whisk well to combine.

In the bowl of a stand mixer fitted with the whisk attachment or in a large bowl using a handheld mixer (or a whisk and a lot of elbow grease), whisk together the eggs, granulated sugar, and jam until light and fluffy, about 2 minutes of aggressive whisking. Whisk the milk into the egg mixture and then gently fold the flour mixture into the liquid mixture. Pour the batter into the prepared baking pan and bake until the cake is springy to the touch, a toothpick tests clean when inserted into the center of the cake, and the top is golden brown, about 30 minutes.

Meanwhile, make the sauce: Place the evaporated milk, brown sugar, butter, vanilla, and salt in a small saucepan set over medium heat. Cook, stirring to dissolve the sugar, until the mixture is smooth and bubbles form around the edges of the pan, about 3 minutes. Turn off the heat and let the sauce sit while the cake finishes baking.

When the cake is done baking, place the pan on a wire rack and use a skewer or chopstick to poke holes all over the surface of the cake (be sure to poke all the way to the bottom of the pan). Carefully and evenly pour the sauce over the surface of the cake. It might seem like a lot of sauce, but it gets absorbed. Let the cake cool to room temperature. Cut into twelve pieces and serve. Spoon any extra sauce from the baking pan over the pieces.

Iced Rooibos Tea with Orange, Cloves, and Cinnamon

Rooibos, which translates to "red bush," is a plant indigenous to South Africa that's used to make herbal tea. The tea has a rusty hue and tastes like a cross between earthy yerba mate tea and flowery hibiscus tea. While many serve it hot with cream and sugar, we like to steep it with cloves and cinnamon, cool it down, mix it with orange juice, and serve it as a refreshing iced tea. Rooibos tea bags are widely available, especially in health food stores, and online from retailers such as rishi-tea.com. If you have extra cinnamon sticks, feel free to use them for garnish.

SERVES 4

2 tablespoons granulated sugar

4 whole cloves

One 2-inch piece cinnamon stick

3 cups water

4 rooibos tea bags

1 cup orange juice

Ice, for serving

1 orange, sliced, for serving

Place the sugar, cloves, cinnamon, and water in a small pot set over high heat and bring to a boil. Stir to dissolve the sugar, turn off the heat, add the tea bags, and let the mixture sit until it cools to room temperature. Pour the mixture through a fine-mesh sieve into a large pitcher (discard the contents of the sieve) and stir in the orange juice. Fill four glasses with ice and orange slices and divide the drink among the glasses. Serve immediately.

Chapter Seven

Madag

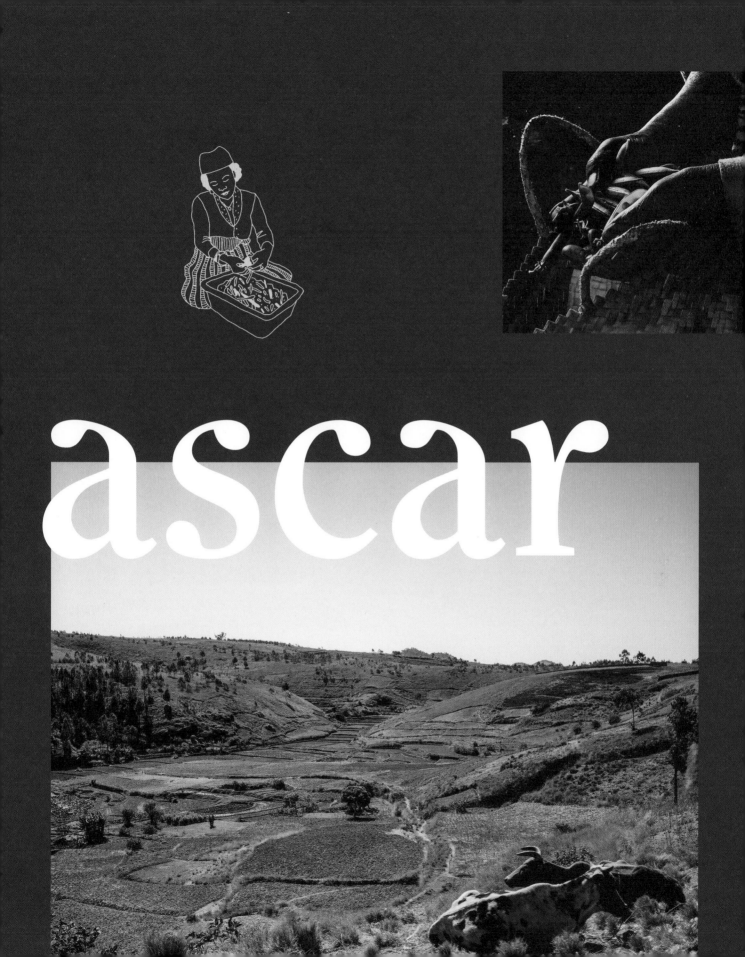

ascar

Madagascar consists of the island of Madagascar and a bunch of small peripheral islands. It split off from the Indian subcontinent over eighty million years ago and was left to sit in complete isolation for almost all those years. This long period of isolation resulted in Madagascar becoming a biodiversity hot spot, meaning a region with high levels of biodiversity that has thrived because humans haven't gotten in the way (though it is now threatened by humans). Almost 90 percent of the plants and animals found in Madagascar cannot be found anywhere else.

Humans first came to Madagascar from Southeast Asia. Migrants from East Africa and the Arabian Peninsula soon joined them. For long periods of time, these groups remained separate. It wasn't until the eighteenth century that they became unified, but because there was so much resistance to unification among the migrant populations, they weren't able to band together to combat the arrival of European colonists.

The French started to colonize Madagascar in 1896, and they ruled through the next century, ceding power only in 1960. It took about fifteen years for the country to transition from colonialism, and in 1975, President Didier Ratsiraka led Madagascar into a socialist system. This ended in 1993, following many years of often-violent protests. Madagascar's modern leadership has had a difficult time not only invigorating its economy but also preserving its biodiversity.

The distinct combination of cultures (including folks with Southeast Asian, East African, Arabian, and European backgrounds) that have come together to create Madagascar and the incredible availability of indigenous ingredients (Madagascar supplies most of the world's vanilla) have not only impacted the culture but have also influenced the cuisine of Madagascar in a myriad of ways.

Geography and Climate

Madagascar is one of the five largest islands in the world and covers 228,900 square miles. It lies about 250 miles off the coast of Mozambique (roughly the distance from New York City to Washington, DC). Mauritius and the French territory of Réunion sit to Madagascar's east, and Comoros and the French territory of Mayotte are to Madagascar's northwest. The eastern highlands and eastern coast are the most densely populated parts of the country, while the western plains remain mostly unpopulated by humans. Madagascar's climate varies, depending on where you are on the island and on which way the monsoon winds blow. Half the year tends to be very wet, starting in November and going through the spring until about April. A cooler, drier season starts in May and lasts until October. The southwest part of Madagascar is dry throughout the year.

Economy and Resources

Plants and animals remain the most remarkable resources in Madagascar. Since the island was long isolated from other continents, almost 90 percent of the plants and animals found in Madagascar cannot be found anywhere else. Some ecologists call Madagascar the world's 8th continent, since it contains so many endemic species. However, this wildlife is being actively threatened by a rapidly growing human population, slash-and-burn agricultural practices, and global warming.

While Madagascar does not have a thriving economy, it does have a lot of promise. It has many natural resources, including coal, uranium, and bauxite. Agriculture and fishing are the economy's mainstays. The amount of arable land and potential gas and oil reserves are also auspicious for future growth. Madagascar is the world's largest supplier of ylang-ylang (a flower prized for its oil), vanilla, and cloves. In fact, Madagascar supplies 80 percent of the world's vanilla. Other major exports include coffee, shrimp, precious and semiprecious stones, and lychees.

People

About twenty-five million people call Madagascar home, and the population is very young. Roughly 40 percent of the population is below the age of fifteen, about half are between fifteen and sixty-four, and only 3 percent are over the age of sixty-five. Madagascar's population is made up almost entirely of eighteen Malagasy ethnic groups.

Language

The most popular languages in Madagascar are Malagasy and French. Malagasy is a Malayo-Polynesian language, which itself is an Austronesian language (Austronesian languages are spoken by almost four hundred million people across island nations in the Pacific Ocean, Southeast Asia, and elsewhere). While Malagasy has always been the national language,

French and English were introduced as official languages in the Constitution of 2007; a November 2010 referendum removed English.

Religion

According to the 1993 census, about half the population of Madagascar practiced Christianity, while the other half practiced traditional religions that centered on honoring ancestors (known as razana). But according to the Pew Research Center, as of 2010, about 85 percent of the population now practices Christianity. The change over the last couple of decades is indicative of the growth of and shifts in the population.

Ma Jeanne

HOME
Sarimanina, Madagascar

HER RECIPES
Carrot Salad with Vinaigrette (page 232)

Tsaramaso Malagasy (Traditional Malagasy White Beans, page 233)

Braised Oxtails (page 238)

How often do you cook?

It depends on how much money we have, but I usually cook about three times a week, and we try to go to the big city to buy ingredients like beans when we can. Sunday, the family is off, and no one is working, so we make good food on Sundays.

Do you enjoy cooking?

[*face lights up*] I do, especially because I'm a mom, I'm a grandmother, and I like making food for my family. I really love to cook rice, beans, cassava [yuca], and bread. I have a feeling to cook.

How many kids do you have?

Five.

And grandchildren?

Four.

Did you teach your children to cook?

I have, even my sons. All my children know how to cook and to do laundry. Two of my children live on the other side of Madagascar, but they visit when they can. They come for Christmas.

Who taught you how to cook?

It's inside of me. I also sometimes follow the television, and there are local channels that show you how to cook, so sometimes I try to cook what they cook. I practice every time that I cook.

What dish best represents Madagascar food?

The main food is bread and beans and rice, and if you have money, you have some meat. Local people will cook beans and meat like this in the middle of the day and also have it for dinner. So, one time cooking but two meals.

Ma Baomaka

HOME
Ambohidratrimo, Madagascar

HER RECIPES
Katilesy (Beef and Potato Fritters, page 239)

Kadaka Akondro (Green Plantains with Braised Beef, page 240)

Mofo Akondro (Banana Fritters, page 241)

What dish best represents Madagascar food?

Chicken soup represents the region where I come from, but cassava [yuca] leaves mixed with pork best represents our country.

How often do you cook, and do you enjoy cooking?

I cook three times a day. I really love cooking. I even cook in my children's houses on weekends because I like cooking for my family.

Do your children and grandchildren cook?

Yes, all of my children cook. My grandchildren don't cook yet, they are so young.

What does passing on food traditions mean to you?

It is my souvenir for them to remember that I existed, but also for them to be able to please their family. Good food makes your family happy, and in my countryside, a woman must know how to cook.

What does home mean to you?

The place where one lives permanently, where family can be secured, and where you can share your sadness and happiness with family.

How do you define community?

Community is a group of people living in a particular local area. For us Malagasy, community is very important.

Looking back, what are you most proud of?

The behavior toward all around me. I always tried to give my best. I like helping people.

Mofo Gasy

(YEASTED RICE AND COCONUT PANCAKES)

Totally gluten-free, these light pancakes are made with soaked and ground rice, a little yeast for leavening, and coconut in three forms—there's coconut milk and shredded coconut in the pancakes, and the pancakes are cooked in coconut oil. While these pancakes are typically made in a special pan that forms them into spheres, we find the batter turns out beautifully when formed into silver dollar–style pancakes, cooked in a regular nonstick skillet. Serve them as is, drizzled with honey (that's how we like them best), dusted with confectioners' sugar, drizzled with maple or palm syrup, or topped with a spoonful of jam. Note that the rice needs to soak for at least 4 hours before cooking, and the batter itself needs about an hour to get the yeast going. Otherwise, they're quite simple to make, and the time-consuming part is totally hands-off.

MAKES ABOUT 40 SMALL PANCAKES

1 cup long-grain white rice (preferably basmati)

1 cup full-fat unsweetened coconut milk

¼ cup unsweetened coconut flakes

¼ cup granulated sugar

1 teaspoon active dry yeast

½ teaspoon kosher salt

½ teaspoon ground cardamom

Coconut oil, for cooking

Honey, for serving (optional)

Place the rice in a fine-mesh sieve and rinse with cold tap water, stirring the rice gently with your hands, until the water runs clear, about 1 minute. Place the rinsed rice in a bowl, cover with cold water, and soak in the refrigerator for at least 4 hours or up to overnight. Drain the rice and place it in the jar of a blender. Add the coconut milk, coconut flakes, sugar, yeast, salt, and cardamom. Puree until smooth. Pour the batter into a large bowl, cover with a clean kitchen towel or plastic wrap, and let it sit in a warm spot in your kitchen until bubbles form on the surface and the batter has risen and is quite thick, about 1 hour.

Place about 2 tablespoons of the coconut oil in a large nonstick skillet set over medium heat and swirl to coat the bottom of the skillet. Once a drop of the batter sizzles on contact, drop spoonfuls of the batter into the skillet to form small pancakes about 2 inches in diameter, leaving plenty of space between them (the exact number will depend on the size of your pan). Cook until the undersides are golden brown, about 2 minutes, then carefully flip each pancake and cook until the second sides are brown, about 1 more minute. Transfer the pancakes to a serving platter, cover with a clean kitchen towel to keep warm, and repeat the process with the remaining batter (add coconut oil to the pan in between batches as necessary). Serve warm, drizzled with honey, if you like.

Carrot Salad with Vinaigrette

This simple carrot salad is a type of laoka, an accompaniment with a meal, just like Lasary Legioma (Tomato Relish, page 234), and it goes well with just about everything. Ma Jeanne serves it with her Tsaramaso Malagasy (Traditional Malagasy White Beans, opposite), Braised Oxtails (page 238), and a big bowl of steaming white rice. She usually makes it on Sundays, when her family is all together.

SERVES 4

3 tablespoons white vinegar, plus more as needed

3 tablespoons canola oil

1 teaspoon granulated sugar, plus more as needed

½ teaspoon kosher salt, plus more as needed

2 large shallots, thinly sliced

4 large carrots, coarsely grated

Place the vinegar, oil, sugar, and salt in a large bowl and whisk well to combine and until the sugar is dissolved. Stir in the shallots and carrots and mix well. Season to taste and feel free to add a little more vinegar, sugar, and/or salt if you'd like. If you have time, let the carrots sit for about 30 minutes at room temperature before serving so the vinaigrette can really soak into the carrots. You can even make it up to 3 days ahead. Just cover the carrots, refrigerate, and bring them back to room temperature before serving. Season the carrots to taste one final time before serving.

Tsaramaso Malagasy

(TRADITIONAL MALAGASY WHITE BEANS)

Ma Jeanne keeps her beans in a tin in her kitchen and regularly cooks them on her stove, which is made of cinder blocks on top of burning wood and charcoal that she maneuvers with intuition earned only by years of experience. If possible, soak your beans overnight before cooking them to help them cook more evenly and to reduce their cooking time. If you don't soak them, no worries; it might just take a little longer to cook them.

SERVES 4

½ pound dried white beans, rinsed well and drained (soak overnight if you have time; see recipe introduction)

Kosher salt

3 large tomatoes (preferably Roma)

¼ cup canola oil

1 large red onion, thinly sliced

Place the beans in a large pot and add enough cold water to cover the beans by an inch. Set the pot over high heat and bring to a boil, then turn the heat as low as it can go and partially cover the pot so steam can escape. Simmer the beans, stirring them every so often, until they're tender, anywhere from 1 to 2 hours, depending on how old they were to begin with. Make sure the beans are covered with water at all times (if too much evaporates, just add a bit more hot water to the pot). Season the beans to taste with salt and drain, reserving 1 cup of their cooking liquid (discard the remaining liquid or reserve for another use such as adding to a soup).

Meanwhile, slice off and discard the tops of the tomatoes and squeeze out and discard the seeds. Thinly slice the tomatoes and set them aside.

Place the oil in a large Dutch oven or other heavy pot and set over medium-high heat. Add the onion and cook, stirring occasionally, until the onion sizzles and starts to take on a little color on the edges, about 2 minutes. Stir in the tomatoes, cover, and cook until the tomatoes begin to break down, about 2 minutes. Stir in the beans with the 1 cup reserved cooking liquid. Cover the pot and bring the mixture to a boil. Uncover and allow the beans to boil until the mixture has thickened significantly but remains soupy, about 10 minutes. Season the beans one final time to taste with salt and serve hot. Leftovers can be stored in an airtight container in the refrigerator for up to a few days and rewarmed in a pot set over low heat (stir while you heat).

Lasary Legioma

(TOMATO RELISH)

Most meals in Madagascar consist of rice served with accompaniments called laoka. Laoka can include anything from fish to vegetables and even condiments like this relish. Not unlike pico de gallo in Mexico, this tomato relish is a mixture of finely chopped tomatoes, mixed with fresh lime, chopped cilantro, a little fresh ginger, and tons of scallions; it's served as a side dish with any and everything in Madagascar. We like it as a topping for grilled fish or shrimp, an omelet filling, or a component in a rice or grain bowl. It's also wonderful served with fresh soft cheeses like feta and ricotta on grilled bread or crackers.

MAKES ABOUT 2 CUPS

3 large tomatoes, finely diced

6 scallions, ends trimmed, thinly sliced

3 tablespoons freshly squeezed lime juice

1 teaspoon minced ginger

½ teaspoon kosher salt

Small handful of cilantro or parsley leaves, minced

Place the tomatoes, scallions, lime juice, ginger, salt, and cilantro in a medium bowl, stir to combine, and let sit at room temperature for at least 20 minutes and up to 2 hours before serving so all the flavors have a chance to marinate together. Leftovers can be stored in a container in the refrigerator for up to 3 days (bring to room temperature and season to taste again before serving).

Akoho Misy Sakamalao

(CHICKEN THIGHS WITH GARLIC, GINGER, AND COCONUT OIL)

These very flavorful chicken thighs are incredibly simple to make. If you have the foresight, let the thighs marinate with the garlic, ginger, and salt in the refrigerator overnight—it will make a noticeable difference. If you don't have time to let the thighs marinate, no worries, they're still great. Cooking them in coconut oil adds tons of flavor. Serve them with cooked rice and a vegetable, like cooked greens or roasted tomatoes. Be sure to spoon the juices from the chicken over your rice.

SERVES 4

2 pounds boneless, skinless chicken thighs

6 garlic cloves, minced

2 tablespoons minced ginger

1 teaspoon kosher salt

2 tablespoons coconut oil

Place the chicken thighs in a large bowl with the garlic and ginger and sprinkle with the salt. Using your hands, rub the aromatics all over the chicken. If you have time, cover the bowl with plastic wrap, place it in the refrigerator, and allow the chicken to marinate for up to 24 hours.

When you're ready to cook the chicken, warm the coconut oil in a large cast-iron skillet or other heavy skillet set over medium-high heat. Add the chicken and cook, turning the pieces occasionally, until deeply browned and cooked through, about 15 minutes. Serve warm. Any leftovers can be stored, covered, in the refrigerator for up to a few days and then rewarmed in a 300°F oven or a skillet set over medium heat for a few minutes.

Braised Oxtails

While Ma Jeanne usually prepares this recipe with zebu meat—a very tough meat from a type of local cattle—we applied that preparation technique to oxtails, which have a similar meat-to-bone ratio and are more readily available in the United States. The meat literally falls off the bone and needs nothing more than cooked rice to soak up all the cooking juices. Speaking of rice, when you cook a pot of rice, do as Ma Jeanne and so many other home cooks in Madagascar do: make ranovola, or burnt rice tea. Scoop all your rice from the pot and leave behind whatever rice sticks to the pot. Let this stuck-on rice cook until it's browned, then fill the pot with water, bring it to a boil, reduce the heat, and let it simmer for an hour or two. Let the liquid cool, then strain it and drink it cold.

SERVES 4

2½ pounds oxtails

Kosher salt

½ cup canola oil

3 cups water

4 large tomatoes (preferably Roma)

2 large red onions, thinly sliced

2 tablespoons granulated sugar

Season the oxtails generously with salt.

Place ¼ cup of the oil in a large Dutch oven or other heavy pot set over high heat. Add the oxtails, working in batches if necessary, depending on the size of your pot, and cook, turning occasionally, until browned all over, about 15 minutes. Add the water and bring to a boil. Reduce the heat to low, partially cover the pot, and simmer the oxtails, stirring them every so often, until tender, about 2 hours.

Meanwhile, slice off and discard the tops of the tomatoes and squeeze out and discard the seeds. Thinly slice the tomatoes and set them aside.

Transfer the oxtails and their cooking liquid to a large bowl and set aside. Add the remaining ¼ cup oil to the pot and set the pot over high heat. Add the onion and cook, stirring occasionally, until the onion sizzles and starts to take on a little color on the edges, about 1 minute. Stir in the tomatoes, cover, and cook until the tomatoes begin to break down, about 1 minute. Return the oxtails and their cooking juices to the pot. Sprinkle with the sugar and stir well to combine. Cook until the liquid has mostly reduced into a thick sauce and coats the oxtails. Serve hot. Leftovers can be stored in an airtight container in the refrigerator for up to a few days and rewarmed in a pot over low heat (stir while you heat).

Katilesy

(BEEF AND POTATO FRITTERS)

Perfect for stretching leftover cooked meat into an entirely new meal, these fritters are best made with meat you have previously cooked, such as Braised Oxtails (opposite) or any type of stewed or braised beef (or any type of meat, for that matter). Simply shred the meat and discard whatever bones are left over and proceed with the recipe. If you are starting from scratch, you can simmer 2 pounds of beef stew meat (preferably on the bone for more flavor) in a little bit of water with some chopped onion and garlic for flavor. Cook until the meat is tender (probably about 2 hours) and then allow it to cool to room temperature before shredding the meat.

MAKES ABOUT 18 FRITTERS

2 large baking potatoes, coarsely chopped

1 pound shredded cooked beef (see recipe introduction)

1 teaspoon kosher salt, plus more as needed

½ teaspoon freshly ground black pepper

2 scallions, ends trimmed, thinly sliced

Large handful of Italian parsley leaves (about ¼ cup), finely chopped

2 cups all-purpose flour

2 large eggs

Canola oil, for frying

Place the potatoes in a medium saucepan, cover with cold water, and set over high heat. Bring to a boil, reduce the heat to low, and simmer until the potatoes are tender, about 15 minutes. Drain the potatoes and place them in a large bowl.

Add the beef to the potatoes and season with the salt and pepper. Use a potato masher or a fork to crush the potatoes and the meat together. Stir in the scallions and parsley. Break off small handfuls of the mixture and roll into golf ball–sized balls with your hands (you should end up with about eighteen balls).

Place the flour on a large plate. Place the eggs in a shallow bowl and beat them well with a fork or a whisk. Coat each meat-potato ball in the flour, then the beaten egg, then return them to the flour for one last coating.

Meanwhile, line a plate with paper towels and set aside. Heat 1 inch of oil in a Dutch oven or other heavy pot set over medium-high heat until the oil reaches 375°F on an instant-read thermometer or until a fritter sizzles on contact. Carefully place the fritters into the hot oil, working in batches as necessary, depending on the size of your pot, and fry, turning the fritters with a slotted spoon as they cook, until they are golden brown all over, about 4 minutes. Carefully transfer the fritters to the prepared plate to drain and then sprinkle with a little bit of salt. Serve hot.

Kadaka Akondro

(GREEN PLANTAINS WITH BRAISED BEEF)

Similar to Ma Josefina's Plantains with Coconut and Prawns (page 188) from Mozambique and Ma Mariama's M'tsolola (Fish, Yuca, Green Plantain, and Coconut Milk Stew, page 266) from Comoros, Ma Baomaka's simple stew makes the most out of a little protein with lots of plantains for heft. While Ma Baomaka uses over a dozen small green plantains that are readily available in Madagascar, we call for just six green plantains, since the ones available in the United States are much larger. You could also use lamb stew meat or goat instead of oxtails. Serve with plain white rice and an accompaniment like Lasary Legioma (Tomato Relish, page 234) or Ma Jeanne's Carrot Salad with Vinaigrette (page 232).

SERVES 4

Kosher salt

2½ pounds oxtails

¼ cup canola oil

1 large yellow onion, coarsely chopped

3 cups water

6 green plantains

2 tablespoons granulated sugar

Season the oxtails generously with salt.

Place the oil in a large Dutch oven or other heavy pot set over high heat. Add the oxtails, working in batches if necessary, depending on the size of your pot, and cook, turning occasionally, until browned all over, about 15 minutes. Add the onion and water to the pot and bring the mixture to a boil. Reduce the heat to low, partially cover the pot, and simmer the oxtails, stirring them every so often, until they're tender, about 2 hours.

Meanwhile, prepare the plantains by first putting on a pair of disposable gloves to keep your hands from getting too sticky while you peel them. Using a paring knife to help you trim the ends and skins, peel. Cut the plantains in half lengthwise and then cut each half in quarters crosswise (you'll end up with eight pieces per plantain). Rinse the plantains in cold water to remove excess starch and then drain them.

Add the plantains to the pot with the meat and sprinkle with the sugar. Stir well to combine, turn the heat on high, and bring the mixture to a boil. Reduce the heat to low, cover the pot, and simmer until the plantains are tender, about 20 minutes. Season to taste with salt and serve immediately. Leftovers can be stored in an airtight container in the refrigerator for up to a few days and rewarmed in a pot set over low heat (stir while you heat).

Mofo Akondro

(BANANA FRITTERS)

Almost like banana tempura, these fritters are made of ripe bananas dipped into a yeasted batter made with cassava flour that's light and crisp. (For more about cassava flour, see page 18.) If you can't find cassava flour, feel free to use all-purpose flour, although that would no longer make these fritters gluten- and grain-free. Serve these as Ma Baomaka does, with hot coffee. In fact, she says you must serve coffee to guests and that it would be wrong to have people come into your home and not serve them freshly roasted and brewed coffee. She makes her coffee just like Ma Gehennet makes hers (see page 54), by roasting green coffee beans in a dry pot and then grinding them and brewing them with hot water. The only difference is that Ma Baomaka builds her own fire to roast the beans and has a granddaughter grind them in a wooden mortar that's the size of a cinder block using a pestle that's taller than she is. (Ma Gehennet, who lives just outside New York City, uses an electric stove and an electric coffee grinder.)

SERVES 4

1½ cups warm water (at body temperature)

1 teaspoon active dry yeast

3 tablespoons granulated sugar, plus extra for serving

1 cup cassava flour or all-purpose flour

4 bananas, sliced on the diagonal into 1-inch-thick pieces

Canola oil, for frying

Place the water and yeast in a medium bowl and stir to combine. Let the mixture sit until the yeast has dissolved and the mixture is cloudy when you stir it, about 5 minutes. Whisk in the sugar and the flour to form a thick, smooth batter. Cover the bowl with a clean kitchen towel and allow the batter to sit until it has thickened and smells yeasty, about 30 minutes.

Meanwhile, line a plate with paper towels and set aside. Heat 1 inch of oil in a Dutch oven or other heavy pot set over medium-high heat until it reaches 375°F on an instant-read thermometer or until a pinch of batter sizzles on contact. Carefully dip the banana slices in the batter, letting the excess drip back into the bowl, and place the fritters into the hot oil, working in batches as necessary, depending on the size of your pot (don't crowd the pot). Fry, turning the fritters with a slotted spoon as they cook, until golden brown all over, about 4 minutes. Carefully transfer the fritters to the prepared plate to drain. Sprinkle with extra sugar, if you'd like, and serve immediately, while hot.

Sliced Papaya with Vanilla Cream

This simple vanilla-infused cream makes ripe papaya even more special than it already is. Try serving the cream on other fruit (it goes especially well on sliced mango, pineapple, and berries). Be sure to throw the whole vanilla pod into the pot with the cream after you scrape the seeds out—the pod itself has a ton of flavor, even if it's not entirely edible. In fact, after the cream, you can rinse it off and place it in a jar, cover with vodka or bourbon, and let it sit in a dark spot to make your own pure vanilla extract. Keep adding pods to the jar after you scrape them for other recipes (such as Grilled Lobster Tails with Vanilla Sauce, page 269), and you'll end up with liquid gold in your cupboard.

SERVES 4

½ cup heavy cream

1 vanilla bean (preferably from Madagascar or Comoros)

2 tablespoons granulated sugar

Pinch of kosher salt

1 large or 2 small papayas, peeled, seeded, and cut into thick slices

Place the cream in a small saucepan set over medium heat. Slice the vanilla bean lengthwise and use the blunt end of a paring knife or a spoon to scrape out the seeds. Place the vanilla seeds and the scraped pod into the pot with the cream and add the sugar and salt. Cook, stirring, until bubbles form at the edges, about 3 minutes. Turn off the heat and let the mixture cool to room temperature. Remove the vanilla pod (see the recipe introduction for a good idea of what to do with it). Place the papaya on a serving platter and evenly spoon the vanilla cream over it. Serve immediately or cover and refrigerate for up to 6 hours before serving, then serve cold.

Ginger Spritz

Homemade ginger beer is popular throughout Madagascar, and our riff on it doesn't require any home brewing or fermentation. A quick blitz of fresh ginger, honey, and lemon (all prominent Malagasy flavors) in the blender makes a really assertive base that goes so well with seltzer or sparkling wine. You could also combine the ginger mixture with boiling water rather than seltzer and serve hot (this is particularly soothing if you have a sore throat or a cold).

SERVES 4

One 2-inch piece ginger, coarsely chopped (no need to peel)

¼ cup honey

¼ cup freshly squeezed lemon juice

½ cup water

4 cups seltzer or sparkling wine

Ice, for serving

Place the ginger, honey, lemon juice, and water in the jar of a blender and puree until smooth. Pour the mixture through a fine-mesh sieve into a pitcher and press down to extract all the flavor from the ginger (discard the contents of the sieve). Stir the seltzer into the pitcher. Fill four glasses with ice and divide the drink among them. Serve immediately.

Chapter Eight

Como

ros

Comoros, a name that derives from *qamar*, the Arabic word for "moon," is an archipelago in the Indian Ocean, situated between Mozambique and Madagascar. Long colonized by the French, the three main islands that make up the country are Ngazidja (known by its French name, Grande Comore), Mwali (also known as Mohéli), and Nzwani (also known as Anjouan), all of which became independent in 1975. The fourth large island in the archipelago, Mayotte, remains a French territory. There are various islets that are also part of the country. Bantu people first inhabited the entire archipelago, and starting in the fifteenth century, it became an important spot for trade among Arab, African, European, and Persian traders. This history has had a lasting effect on the food prepared throughout the islands. You'll find hints of influence from all these places in the recipes, plus the use of indigenous ingredients such as coconuts and spices.

Geography and Climate

Situated at the northern end of the Mozambique Channel between Mozambique and Madagascar, Comoros consists of volcanic islands, surrounded by the vast Indian Ocean. The capital, Moroni, is also the islands' largest city. Other major cities include Domoni, Fomboni, Mutsamudu, and Tsémbéhou. Comoros is one of the smallest countries in the world. Its islands were formed through volcanic activity, and active volcanoes such as Mount Karthala, located on Ngazidja (Grande Comore), continue to be a part of the landscape (Mount Karthala is also one of the most active volcanoes in the world). Comoros's climate resembles that of Mozambique—it's tropical, and the first half of the year is rainy.

Economy and Resources

Comoros is among the world's poorest countries. Agriculture is the leading sector of the economy, and nearly half of Comoros's exports are spices. While other island countries in the Indian Ocean, like the Seychelles and Mauritius, have thrived on tourism, Comoros has not yet built the infrastructure to support a large influx of tourists. Its main exports include ylang-ylang, cloves, and vanilla.

People

Comoros is home to fewer than a million people, but its citizens live very closely together. Its population is also quite young, and almost half of Comoros's citizens are under the age of fifteen. Most have African Arab origins, including many with Shirazi roots. Malagasy and Indian citizens descend from French settlers. Although many French citizens left following independence, some have remained.

Language

Comorian (also known as Shikomori) is the most common language spoken in Comoros, and it has four different variants that are all related to Swahili. The variants include Shimaore, Shinzwani, Shingazidja, and Shimwali. French and Arabic are also official languages in Comoros.

Religion

Nearly the entire population of Comoros practices Sunni Islam (the largest denomination of Muslims). It is the only Muslim-majority country in southern Africa. A small minority of Comoros's population, made up mostly of immigrants from France, practices Roman Catholicism.

Salimani ya Itsandra, Grande Comore

Ma Zakia

HOME
Moroni, Comoros

HER RECIPE
Roho (Comorian Wedding Sweet, page 272)

What did you choose to make today?

Roho. I chose to make it because it's really representative of our gastronomy and something we serve at weddings, and usually at weddings we only serve very special things. It's not mainstream. It makes me feel special because it's not something everyone does, or can, make. It feels like it holds value.

Where did roho come from?

It's a very old dish. Ancient Comorians used to cook this, and not every country cooks this. It's very special to here.

And who makes the best version of it?

My mother makes the best version of everything, so everything I make is the second best!

How often do you cook?

I used to cook very often, but now I feel more tired and weak, so I only cook on special occasions.

Do your children and grandchildren cook?

My grandchildren aren't old enough to cook, but my children have watched me cook so they know how to cook. It rejoices me to share something, to cook something that is a success with my family. It makes me happy.

What does home mean to you?

It's where I have my habits. It's where I feel complete. When I go elsewhere, I feel uncomfortable. At home, I know *this is my kitchen, this is my bed*.

How do you define community?

Being together, helping each other, giving counsel and advice and consolation to each other.

What was your favorite meal growing up?

I can't remember. I've always liked everything. I am a foodie! I love everything. This is a difficult question.

What are your hopes for women in your community?

I would like to see women go forward to have positions in society and to have important roles and responsibilities, especially in the ways they educate their children. Women should be leading education. It's important to me that women carry themselves well and dress well and respect themselves.

What does it mean to be a woman in Comoros?

It's about being dedicated to taking care of children. You have your children, and you take care of them, and then you have your grandchildren and you take care of them. So, you don't really have space for yourself and your own projects. It's a bit of a shame sometimes because you don't really have time to relax.

Ma Mariama

HOME
Salimani, Itsandra, Grande Comore

HER RECIPE
M'tsolola (Fish, Yuca, Green Plantain, and Coconut Milk Stew, page 266)

Why did you choose to make m'tsolola to share with us?

Because it's a traditional thing here. You have to cook bananas in Comoros—bananas are very important, and coconut is, too. I decided to do this because it would've been longer to cook the ntsambou [a labor-intensive dish made of dried and fermented nuts], which is very traditional, but this is faster.

What dish best represents Comorian food?

I always say ntsambou, but I didn't have the time to make it. It's very labor-intensive.

What is most misunderstood about Comoros?

[*sighs*] This is a hard question.

When you go to another country and say you're a Comorian, how do people react?

People say, "Your country is 100 percent Muslim, but then you have a lot of people drinking in your country," so I say, yes, we have people drinking, but it's a practice that was imported, and people who drink still go to the mosque, so they're still Muslim. We were colonized by the French, so there were some practices we adopted.

How often do you cook, and do you enjoy cooking?

I cook every day, and I can make a lot of things. I can make Swahili food, Arab food, Chinese food. I love it. I didn't study it, but God gave me this gift, and I love cooking, and I am grateful for that.

Do your children and grandchildren cook?

My daughter loves cooking, and I myself learned from my grand-mother. My daughter even went to school to learn how to cook and to learn about tourism. Unfortunately, she hasn't found a job yet, so I told her maybe she should push hard to open her own thing and to start working for herself.

What does passing on food traditions mean to you?

I really enjoy teaching people, every kind of people, and it's a pleasure. It's really rewarding.

When I do something for someone, like if someone asks me to cook something for them, I am very grateful because people always say, "It was good" or "You made it good." Even if they don't pay me, I am grateful because everything I'm doing now, I will be rewarded by God. So even if I'm not paid, it's still very rewarding for me.

What does home mean to you?

Home, for me, is my village. Even though I was born in the medina [the town], I still consider myself a woman from my village.

How do you define community?

It's like love. It's when you love someone. Like I didn't know you, but now I love you. You are part of my community.

Looking back, what are you most proud of?

I am proud of everything I've done.

Can you share one moment when you were really proud?

When I traveled and I brought back furniture, and my father could sit on the couch. I was very proud that my father was sitting in my living room on my couch, and I had made an effort to earn money and be able to bring the furniture home. Another thing was that my father died in my hands. I feel like I took care of him until he died.

What was your favorite meal growing up?

[*laughs*] Ntsambou.

That's why you're so obsessed with it!

One time it even made me sick. My aunt cooked it. But before, people wouldn't eat until their husbands were home, and then the husbands would eat first. So, we had to wait until her husband came. I had to wait so long that I felt sick. It felt like he broke my heart making me wait! I had to go to the doctor.

Who decides what to cook in your house?

Traditionally, it's not the place of a woman to decide what we're going to cook. It's usually the husband or the brother or the father. Now more and more things are changing. For me, it's a bit of a shame because it's not the way things used to be, and it's in our traditions and in our religion.

What do you think of young people like us who believe in women's rights?

If you don't have a husband, then you have to take the lead!

Sweet Pea Soup with Coconut and Ginger

Coconuts are widely available throughout Comoros, and you will find them used in all sorts of dishes, including soups like this one, which is both easy to make and impressive to serve. The coconut milk not only offers the soup great flavor but also makes it very creamy without using any dairy, adding it to the list of wonderful vegan recipes in this book, such as Ma Gehennet's Shiro (Ground Chickpea Stew, page 45) and Kunde (Black-Eyed Peas and Tomatoes in Peanut Sauce, page 127).

SERVES 4

2 tablespoons canola oil

1 small yellow onion, finely diced

2 tablespoons minced ginger

2 garlic cloves, minced

½ teaspoon cayenne pepper

1 teaspoon kosher salt, plus more as needed

2 cups water

One 13.5-ounce can full-fat unsweetened coconut milk

One 10-ounce package frozen peas

Small handful of cilantro leaves, for serving (optional)

Warm the oil in a medium saucepan set over medium heat. Add the onion, ginger, garlic, cayenne, and salt to the saucepan and cook, stirring occasionally, until the onion is softened, about 10 minutes. Add the water and the coconut milk and increase the heat to high. Once the mixture comes to a boil, reduce the heat to low and add the peas. Cook just until the peas are bright green and tender, about 5 minutes. Puree the soup using an immersion blender or in the jar of a regular blender. Season the soup to taste with salt and ladle into bowls. Top with cilantro leaves, if you like. Serve immediately. Leftovers can be stored in an airtight container in the refrigerator for up to a few days and rewarmed in a pot set over low heat (stir while you heat).

Ambrevades au Curry

(CURRIED PIGEON PEAS)

What we know as pigeon peas in the United States were first cultivated in India thousands of years ago, and they have since found their way to many countries. Known as toor dal in Hindi, gandules throughout Latin America, gungo peas in Jamaica, kardis in Malawi, and ambrevades in French, pigeon peas are a staple of so many cultures. This dish, eaten all over Comoros, takes its name from the French language (a leftover of such a long French hold on the country) and its flavors from the spices and coconut ubiquitous in Comoros. It's an affordable, filling dish that makes for a lovely side or a main meal served over rice. You could do plain rice or something even more flavorful like Bariis (Basmati Rice Pilaf with Raisins, page 87). While pigeon peas are readily available in grocery stores, if you can't find them for any reason, feel free to substitute black-eyed peas.

SERVES 6

3 tablespoons canola oil

2 teaspoons ground cumin

2 teaspoons ground turmeric

½ teaspoon ground cardamom

2 medium vine-ripened tomatoes, coarsely chopped

Kosher salt

Two 15-ounce cans green pigeon peas, drained and rinsed

1 cup full-fat unsweetened coconut milk

Warm the oil in a medium saucepan set over medium heat. Add the cumin, turmeric, and cardamom and cook just until fragrant, about 30 seconds. Add the tomatoes and a large pinch of salt and cook, stirring occasionally, until the tomatoes are nearly dry, about 5 minutes. Add the peas and coconut milk, bring the mixture to a boil, then reduce the heat to low, cover, and cook just long enough to infuse the peas with all the flavor, about 5 minutes. Season the peas to taste with salt and serve hot. Leftovers can be stored in an airtight container in the refrigerator for up to a few days and rewarmed in a pot set over low heat (stir while you heat).

Roti ya Houma Pampa

(SALT COD WITH TOMATOES AND ONIONS)

Fresh cod that has been preserved with salt and air-dried for a time is known as salt cod. It is not dissimilar from other salted, dried proteins like prosciutto, country ham, and all types of jerky. You can find salt cod all over the world (unsurprisingly, it travels well!), and it's a great thing to keep in your pantry, since it's an affordable way of incorporating flavor and protein into your meals and a great way to enjoy fish if fish is not regularly available where you live. Note that you need to plan ahead a bit when preparing it. The cod needs a very long soak before you cook it so that it isn't too salty or too tough to eat. Look for salt cod in the seafood department of your grocery store (it's often in the refrigerated section) or at your local seafood store.

SERVES 4

1 pound boneless salt cod (sometimes labeled saltfish, bacalao, or baccalà)

3 tablespoons canola oil

2 garlic cloves, minced

1 teaspoon ground turmeric

2 yellow onions, thinly sliced into half-moons

4 large tomatoes, coarsely chopped

½ teaspoon freshly ground black pepper

Rinse the salt cod well under running water and rub off any salt on the surface. Place the cod in a large container or bowl, cover with fresh water, and place a plate or something else on top to keep the cod submerged. Cover the container and place it in the refrigerator. Soak, draining and changing the water every 6 hours, for at least 24 hours and up to 48 hours. When you're ready to cook, rinse off the cod, pat it dry, and set it aside while you get your aromatics going.

Place the oil in a large heavy pot or Dutch oven set over medium heat. Add the garlic and turmeric and cook, stirring occasionally, until very fragrant, about 1 minute. Add the onion and cook, stirring occasionally, until beginning to soften, about 5 minutes. Stir in the tomatoes and pepper and increase the heat to high. When the tomatoes start to bubble, immediately reduce the heat to low, set the cod on top of the tomato mixture, and cover. Cook until the cod flakes easily when poked with a spoon or fork, about 10 minutes. Break the fish into large pieces with a serving spoon and serve immediately while hot. Leftovers can be stored in an airtight container in the refrigerator for up to a few days and rewarmed in a pot set over low heat (stir while you heat).

M'tsolola

(FISH, YUCA, GREEN PLANTAIN, AND COCONUT MILK STEW)

Creamy coconut milk and a fiery chile-and-garlic paste are the secrets to m'tsolola, a simple stew that stretches a little fish with a lot of plantains and yuca (also known as cassava; see page 22 for more information). M'tsolola is one of the most consumed dishes throughout Comoros and is considered a meal to be shared; it is usually served in a wide dish called a sinia. Ma Mariama demonstrated how she makes it in her outdoor kitchen; watching her prepare it is a testament to how much physical work cooking often is for women around the world. Rather than turn a knob on a stove, she built a fire. Rather than open a can of coconut milk, she cracked a fresh coconut open with a machete, grated the meat, massaged it with water almost as if she were kneading dough, and strained it to make fresh coconut milk. Rather than throw some chile peppers and garlic cloves in a food processor or even chop them on a cutting board on a counter, she placed them on a large, flat rock on the ground and used a smaller rock to grind them into a paste. We've adapted the recipe slightly to make it more conducive to Western kitchens. In making it, we're reminded how many conveniences we have and how important it is to appreciate them and the effortlessness we're so regularly afforded. A few notes about some of our changes: Ma Mariama uses a banana leaf to keep the stew from boiling over, and she says it also lends a sweet flavor to the broth. It's okay if you don't have one—the stew will still be wonderful. Also, she used very small green plantains that aren't available in the United States, so instead, we call for four large green plantains in their place. Wherever in the world you make this, make it for friends or family. As Ma Mariama told us, "Wageni ni baraka," which means "Guests are a blessing."

SERVES 6 TO 8

2 hot chile peppers (such
as habaneros or jalapeños),
stemmed

1 tablespoon kosher salt, plus
more as needed

3 large garlic cloves

¼ cup freshly squeezed lime juice

2 pounds tuna steaks or other
firm, oily fish (such as mackerel),
cut into 2-inch pieces

4 green plantains

2 pounds yuca (also labeled
cassava), tough brown outer layer
peeled off and discarded, thinly
sliced

2 cups water

1 small red onion, finely diced

1 large banana leaf (optional)

Two 13-ounce cans full-fat
unsweetened coconut milk

Place the chiles and salt in a mortar and use a pestle to grind them to a paste (or place in a small food processor and pulse until finely chopped). Add the garlic, one clove at a time, and grind it into the chile paste. Stir in the lime juice. Place the fish in a large bowl and add the chile paste. Using your hands, rub the paste all over the fish, taking care not to touch your face after handling the hot paste. Cover the bowl and set the fish aside while you prepare the plantains and yuca (you can leave the fish at room temperature for up to 30 minutes or refrigerate for up to 24 hours).

Prepare the plantains by first putting on a pair of disposable gloves to keep your hands from getting too sticky while you peel them. Using a paring knife to help you trim the ends and skins, peel the plaintains. Cut the plantains in half lengthwise and then cut each half in quarters crosswise (you'll end up with eight pieces per plantain). Place the plantains in a large bowl of cold water to preserve their color and to help remove excess starch. Add the yuca to the bowl, mix the plantains and yuca by hand, and set aside.

Place the fish in a large heavy pot with the water. Cover, set the pot over high heat, and cook until steam is pushing its way out from under the lid, about 10 minutes. Use a slotted spoon to transfer the fish to a large plate.

Drain the plantains and yuca and place half of them into the pot with the fish broth. Place the fish and red onion on top and then cover with the remaining plantains and yuca. If you have a banana leaf, rinse it and then cover the pot with it. Whether or not you're using the banana leaf, cover the pot with a lid and bring the mixture back to a boil over high heat. Boil the stew until the plantains and yuca are just tender, about 20 minutes. Uncover the pot, add the coconut milk, and bring the stew back to a boil. Once it boils, turn off the heat. Season the stew to taste with salt. Serve immediately. Leftovers can be stored in an airtight container in the refrigerator for up to a few days and rewarmed in a pot set over low heat (stir while you heat).

Grilled Lobster Tails with Vanilla Sauce

Known throughout Comoros by its French name, langouste à la vanille, this luxurious dish is the national dish of Comoros and features the vanilla that the French started growing in the area just before the twentieth century. Sometimes it's made by simmering lobsters in vanilla sauce, and other times it's made by stuffing whole lobsters with vanilla beans before grilling them. But it's most often made with simply grilled lobster, drizzled with sauce. We just went with lobster tails, since they're more readily available (plus, they're easier to eat than an entire lobster). For the sauce, use whatever white wine you would drink with this (that way, the bottle is already open!). If you don't have an outdoor grill, you can grill the lobster tails on the stovetop in a grill pan.

SERVES 4

Four 6- to 7-ounce lobster tails

Kosher salt

2 tablespoons canola oil

2 tablespoons unsalted butter

2 large shallots, minced

½ cup white wine

1 vanilla bean (preferably from Madagascar or Comoros)

½ cup heavy cream

Prepare an outdoor grill (charcoal, gas, or whatever you have) for medium-high heat. Using a chef's knife, split the lobster tails in half lengthwise, season the cut sides generously with salt, and rub all over with the oil. Grill the lobster tail pieces, turning them every couple of minutes, until the flesh side is nicely charred and the meat is firm to the touch, about 8 minutes. Transfer the lobster tail pieces to a serving platter and cover with aluminum foil to keep them warm.

Meanwhile, place the butter in a small saucepan set over medium heat (you can do this directly on your grill as long as your saucepan is entirely heat-safe). Once the butter has melted, add the shallots and cook, stirring occasionally, until just softened, about 3 minutes. Add the wine, bring the mixture to a boil, and reduce the heat to low (or move the pot to a less intense part of the grill). Slice the vanilla bean lengthwise and, using the blunt end of a paring knife or a spoon, scrape out the seeds. Place the vanilla seeds and the scraped pod in the pot and add the cream and a pinch of salt. Cook, stirring, until bubbles form at the edges, about 3 minutes. Turn off the heat, remove the vanilla pod (see page 17 for a good idea of what to do with it), and season the sauce to taste with salt. Drizzle the sauce over the grilled lobster tail pieces and serve immediately.

Sweet Vermicelli Noodles with Cardamom and Butter

Toasted, softened sweet noodles flavored with cardamom and butter, this dessert is basically a warm noodle pudding. It's cozy and comforting and reminiscent of the many desserts made with toasted vermicelli noodles that are popular all over South Asian countries, whose cuisines have heavily influenced Comoros and beyond. Look for vermicelli noodles made of wheat (not rice) in the pasta aisle at your grocery store or in Indian grocery stores. If you find ones that are already toasted, you can follow the recipe as is for even more toasted flavor or simply just cook the noodles for a minute before adding the water. The easiest and least-messy way to break up the noodles is to crush them in a bag with your hands or a rolling pin (use the bag they came in or transfer them from their package to a plastic bag).

SERVES 4

4 green cardamom pods

3 tablespoons unsalted butter or ghee

6 ounces wheat vermicelli noodles, broken into 2-inch pieces (about 1½ cups)

2 cups boiling water

⅓ cup granulated sugar

Pinch of kosher salt

Use the flat side of a knife or a pestle to lightly crush the cardamom pods. Place the butter in a medium saucepan or large skillet set over medium heat. Once the butter has melted, add the crushed cardamom and vermicelli and cook, stirring occasionally, until the noodles are browned and the butter smells nutty, about 4 minutes. Add the water, sugar, and salt and cook, stirring occasionally, until the vermicelli is tender and almost all the water has been absorbed, about 7 minutes. Serve immediately, while hot, and discard the cardamom pods as you eat.

Roho

(COMORIAN WEDDING SWEET)

Comorian weddings are a huge deal, to say the least, and roho, a fudgelike sweet made of cardamom-infused eggs and sugar, is a special treat often made for these celebrations. It is usually served with strong coffee poured into small cups. Roho must be stirred constantly while cooking. Don't discard the leftover egg whites; save them in the refrigerator for a day or two to add to your next omelet or to whip and fold into cake or pancake batter.

MAKES 16 SQUARES

5 large eggs

5 large egg yolks

2 cups granulated sugar

1 cup ghee, at room temperature

1 teaspoon ground cardamom

½ cup sweetened condensed milk

Place the eggs and egg yolks in a large heavy pot and whisk well to combine. Whisk in the sugar, ghee, cardamom, and condensed milk (it's okay if the ghee is lumpy at this point—it will melt when you heat the mixture in just a moment). Set the pot over medium-low heat and cook, stirring constantly with a wooden spoon, until thickened and the consistency is like pudding or porridge, about 1 hour. (The fat from the ghee and the egg yolks will start to draw out from the mixture, almost frying the mixture in its own fat; ultimately, the mixture will become less smooth and more granular and will take on a dark caramel color.) Adjust the heat as you cook to keep the roho from burning.

Carefully transfer the mixture to an 8-inch square baking pan. Using a spoon, spread the mixture so that it's in an even layer about ½ inch thick.

While the roho is still hot, using a paring knife, score the top of the mixture in four even strips in both directions (you will have a total of sixteen squares). Let the roho cool to room temperature before cutting into (crumbly) squares along the scored lines and serving. Leftovers can be stored in an airtight container in the refrigerator for up to a week. Serve cold or bring to room temperature before serving.

Watermelon Juice with Lime, Ginger, and Mint

While watermelons originated across the continent in West Africa, they are widely consumed on the eastern coast and on the islands off the coast. Blended with fresh lime juice, spicy ginger, and mint and served over ice, this drink is an ideal way to cool down in hot weather. If you'd like to turn this juice into a cocktail, simply add a splash of rum, tequila, vodka, or gin.

SERVES 4

8 cups seedless watermelon cubes

½ cup freshly squeezed lime juice

One 2-inch piece ginger, peeled and coarsely chopped

12 large mint leaves

Ice, for serving

Place the watermelon, lime juice, ginger, and mint in the jar of a blender and puree until smooth. Fill four tall glasses with ice and divide the drink among them. Serve immediately.

ACKNOWLEDGMENTS

It takes a village to do most things, including to make a book.

First, thank you to each woman who welcomed us into her home, spoke to us, cooked for us, shared a story, and shared a recipe (or a few recipes!).

With thanks to the following people and organizations who helped connect the dots between the bibis and us in so many different ways: In Eritrea: Astu Tilahun, Danait Beyene, Gabriella Mengstab, Lilai Teckie, and Michael Andeberhan. In Somalia: Abdi Latif Ega, Abdul Karim Mohamed, Beverly Hampton, Duran Ahmed Adan, Eman Bare, and Evelyne Wangui Njoroge. In Kenya: Abubakr Dumbuya, Ali Farah, Ciku Muriuki, Gina Din-Kariuki, Hakim Abdalla of Maskani Youth Initiative, Kaniaru Wacieni, Mohammed J. Farah, Samia Omar Bwana of Halal Safaris, Wambui Kinya, and Wangeci Gitobu. In Tanzania: Justa Lujwangana, Kathleen Bomani, and Neema J. Ngelime. In Mozambique: Chike Eleazu, Dag Roll-Hansen, Nuno Santos, and Tamára Ramos. In South Africa: Benjamin J. P. Henecka and Faith Nseula. In Madagascar: Ramartour Madagascar. In Comoros: Shainess Daoud.

Thanks to all who helped make the images in the book: Khadija M. Farah and Jennifer May (with a special shout-out to Chris and Robin for their support!) for taking the photos. Your commitment to the book has meant the world. Thank you to Victoria Campbell for stepping in in Minneapolis (and thank you to Sarah Hrudka for connecting us). Thank you to Jasmine Arielle Ting for being part of the first food shoot and being a real help. Thank you to Dina Nur Satti and Lail Design for loaning us beautiful pieces (check them out at @nur_ceramics and @lail.design), Stephanie Charlene Ceramics and Jane Herold Pottery (@stephanie_charlene and @janeheroldpottery) for discounting their ceramics for us, and Fahari Bazaar (@faharibazaar) and Breakthrough African Market in Albany, New York, for being the source of so many fabrics in the images. And thank you to Araki Koman for her work on the map and illustrations.

Thanks to everyone at Ten Speed Press for believing in the book, giving it your attention and thoughtfulness, and helping us get it out into the world. Special thanks to Dervla Kelly, our champion from day one, as well as Emma Campion, Isabelle Gioffredi, Serena Sigona, Brianne Sperber, and Windy Dorresteyn.

Thank you to Kari Stuart (and thank you to Cat Shook!) for taking this book from dream to reality and for helping us find the right partner.

And thank you to Dr. Jessica B. Harris, Osayi Endolyn, and Howie Kahn for your support.

From Hawa

To my mother: The Prophet Muhammad said, "Paradise is at the feet of the mother." You are the light of our lives, and our anchor. My siblings and I are so lucky to have been born to you—a community organizer, an entrepreneur, a woman of deep faith, and the best mother of all. Thank you for showing me what it means to walk with dignity and integrity. *Waan ku jeclahay, Hooyo*.

To my best friends Giovanni, Joe, Nunu, Mulu, and Shelia: Having you beside me has gotten me through some of my darkest days. Your everlasting kindness has helped me live my wildest dreams. Thank you for the loyalty, friendship, and uninhibited joy you bring to my life. I look forward to riding many more waves together.

To my siblings: I'm so thankful for the stories we've lived through together. Thank you for your unwavering support. It means the world to me. I love you.

To my godchildren: You girls are the greatest joy of my life. Remember, the sky is not the limit.

INDEX

Published in the United States by Ten Speed Press, an imprint of the Crown Publishing Group, a division of Penguin Random House LLC, New York.

www.crownpublishing.com

www.tenspeed.com

Ten Speed Press and the Ten Speed Press colophon are registered trademarks of Penguin Random House LLC.

Library of Congress Cataloging-in-Publication Data

Names: Hassan, Hawa, 1982–author. | Turshen, Julia, author. | Farah, Khadija M., photographer. | May, Jennifer, photographer.

Title: In Bibi's kitchen : the recipes and stories of grandmothers from the eight African countries that touch the Indian Ocean / Hawa Hassan and Julia Turshen ; photography by Khadija M. Farah and Jennifer May.

Description: Emeryville : Ten Speed Press, 2020. | Includes index.

Identifiers: LCCN 2020003798 (print) | LCCN 2020003799 (ebook) | ISBN 9781984856739 (hardcover) | ISBN 9781984856746 (ebook)

Subjects: LCSH: Cooking, Eastern African. | Cooking—Africa, Eastern. | Cooking—Indian Ocean Region. | Women—Africa, Eastern—Interviews. | Grandmothers—Africa, Eastern—Interviews. | Africa, Eastern—Description and travel. | Indian Ocean Region—Description and travel. | LCGFT: Cookbooks.

Classification: LCC TX725.A354 H37 2020 (print) | LCC TX725.A354 (ebook) | DDC 641.59676--dc23

LC record available at https://lccn.loc.gov/2020003798
 LC ebook record available at https://lccn.loc.gov/2020003799

Hardcover ISBN: 9781984856739

eBook ISBN: 9781984856746

Printed in China

Design by Isabelle Gioffredi

10 9 8 7 6 5 4 3 2 1

First Edition